Challenger 6

SECOND EDITION

ADULT READING SERIES

Corea Murphy

New Readers Press

Acknowledgments:

Voices from the Great Depression: From *Hard Times: An Oral History of the Great Depression*, by Studs Terkel. Copyright © 1970 by Studs Terkel. Reprinted by permission of Pantheon Books, a Division of Random House, Inc.

When John Quincy Adams Lost His Job: From *The Bold Brahmins* by Lawrence Lader. Adapted with permission of the author.

Adaptation of "The Automobile Revolution" from *The Big Change: America Transforms Itself 1900–1950* by Frederick Lewis Allen. Copyright 1952 by Frederick Lewis Allen. Reprinted by permission of Harper & Row Publishers, Inc.

Caught in Traffic: Adapted from "Mammon and the Archer" by O. Henry with permission of Airmont Publishing Company, Inc., New York, NY.

A Ride in Space: Condensed and adapted from "Sally Ride: Ready for Liftoff" by Jerry Adler and Pam Abramson. Copyright 1983 by Newsweek, Inc. All rights reserved. Reprinted by permission.

Cartoon p. 124: © 1983 Jim Borgman—*Cincinnati Enquirer.* Reprinted with the permission of King Features Syndicate, Inc.

New York to France—in a Rowboat: Adapted from "New York to France—in a Rowboat" by Tom Mahoney. Copyright © 1948 by Esquire Associates.

As American as Apple Pie: Adapted from *Apples: History, Folklore, Horticulture, and Gastronomy* by Peter Wynne. Copyright © 1975 by Peter Wynne. Used by permission of Dutton, a division of Penguin Group (USA) Inc.

A Breakfast Scene: From *A Raisin in the Sun* by Lorraine Hansberry. Copyright © 1958 by Robert Nemiroff, as an unpublished work. Copyright © 1959, 1966, 1984 by Robert Nemiroff. Copyright renewed 1986, 1987 by Robert Nemiroff. Used by permission of Random House, Inc.

Adaptation of "The Wizard of Tuskegee" from *The Secret Life of Plants* by Peter Tompkins & Christopher Bird. Copyright © 1973 by Peter Tompkins. Reprinted by permission of Harper & Row, Publishers, Inc.

More Facts about the Peanut: Adapted from *The World Book Encyclopedia.* © 1987 World Book, Inc. Reprinted by permission of World Book, Inc.

"To Look at Any Thing" from *The Living Seed,* copyright © 1961 by John Moffitt and renewed 1989 by Henry Moffitt, reprinted by permission of Houghton Mifflin Publishing Company.

Images courtesy of:

p. 7, p. 8 p. 9, p. 15, p. 22, p. 34, p. 36, p. 60, p. 61, p. 71, p. 80, p. 105, p. 106, p. 112, p. 128, p. 141, p. 143, p. 151, p. 152, p. 176, peanuts, p. 178: © 2008 Jupiterimages Corporation; p. 27, p. 41, p. 73, p. 79, p. 106, p. 167, p. 168: istockphoto.com; p. 21, p. 47, p. 53, p. 97, p. 176, George Washington Carver: Public Domain (Wikimedia Commons); p. 120, p. 121: NASA

Challenger 6, 2nd Edition
ISBN 978-1-56420-573-5

Printed in the United States of America
9 8 7 6 5

Proceeds from the sale of New Readers Press materials support professional development, training, and technical assistance programs of ProLiteracy that benefit local literacy programs in the U.S. and around the globe.

Developmental Editor: Terrie Lipke
Contributing Writers: Barbara Hesselgrave, Terry Ledyard, Nina Shope
Creative Director: Andrea Woodbury
Production Specialist: Maryellen Casey
Art and Design Supervisor: James P. Wallace
Cover Design: Carolyn Wallace

Table of Contents

Family. No matter how you define it, everyone has one. In this unit, you will be taking a look at what makes a family a family—and how to keep your family a safe, happy, and healthy one.

The first selection, "Healthy Food, Healthy Family," gives a short history of why today's families may be struggling more with getting and staying on the road to good health than families of the past did. It presents fun and easy ways for any family to take that first step toward a healthier lifestyle.

The face of the American family has changed dramatically over the last few hundred years. In "An American Family Portrait," we'll explore cultural and ethnic diversity as it relates to today's families, and talk about one U.S. agency whose job is to stay on top of these changes as they continue to occur.

Having a baby is near the top of the list as one of life's biggest events. But what if it's twins—or triplets? Lesson 3, "Life with Multiples," presents a quick background and description of how multiple births occur. And it delves into what life with multiples is really like.

Lesson 4, "Lunch with Grandma Janey," presents a multi-generational look at aging. It touches on how dealing with aging or chronically ill family members can affect even the youngest generation.

Everyone wants to save money for that "rainy day." But in today's world, few of us are actually able to do it. The last lesson of the unit, "How to Spend Less and Have More Fun," gives practical tips on how families can cut down on their money worries while finding new ways to enjoy life without spending a fortune.

Words for Study

variety	cholesterol	participate	portions
obesity	Hispanics	nutrition	nutritious
scientists	African Americans	label	absolutely
obese	convenience	calories	specialists
diabetes	novelty	carbohydrates	metabolism

LESSON 1
Healthy Food, Healthy Family

When it comes to eating, we all love to eat. We are also very lucky. This country has enough food, and lots of variety, like fruits and vegetables, dairy products, and meats. We all know these foods are good for you. But there are also plenty of snack foods that are not so good for you. Some of the foods we like the best may not be the best foods for our bodies. Next time you go shopping, look at all the choices we have—good and not so good.

Many people choose foods that are not good for them. Health experts are worried that Americans are getting too heavy. They say Americans of all ages are much fatter now than they were in 1980. A serious weight problem is called obesity. This is now common in kids ages 5 to 15. Scientists say at least 9 million kids are obese.

Why is this a serious problem? First, scientists predict that overweight children will become overweight adults. Second, overweight children and overweight adults can have serious health problems. Diseases like diabetes, high blood pressure, and high cholesterol are very common in the obese. Some people, such as Hispanics and African Americans, can have special medical problems when they are overweight.

Why are Americans getting too big? What made us fat? Let's look back in time and see what happened.

A hundred years ago there were fewer choices of food. There were no fast-food chains, and no huge superstores. There were no corner convenience stores selling sodas and snacks and no drive-throughs offering "supersized meals." People went to the butcher for meat. They went to the outdoor markets for vegetables and fruits. Then they went to the bakery for breads. They had to go lots of places to buy food. Milk, butter, eggs, and cheese were delivered by the milkman. Each night you left a note on the porch. The milkman left your order there the next morning. Most people didn't have refrigerators, so they had to shop every day. But, many people had some kind of garden to grow fresh fruit and vegetables. In places with cold winters, you could only do that in summer.

Then, things changed as more roads were built, railroads were improved, and airlines started flying across the country. Fresh foods could be delivered thousands of miles away from the farm. Oranges from sunny Florida could arrive by truck in snowy Chicago in just a few days. Fresh fish from Maryland shores could go quickly to Kansas by plane. Grocery stores grew bigger each year. Now, you could go to a big store and buy almost everything you needed in one place.

Well, you might think with all these choices people would be healthier than ever before. But then, something else happened. It was called television. When TVs became widely available in the 1950s, most people could not wait to buy one. By 1955 half the families in America owned one TV set. About the same time, a man named Gerry Thomas invented a frozen meal. He called this the "TV Dinner." All you had to do was take it out of the freezer, and put it in the oven to heat. Now, families would sit down and eat while they watched TV. It was a novelty back then. Today, it is very common to eat while watching DVDs or TV shows, or working on the computer. Scientists say

Americans aren't getting much exercise with all this sitting and eating. They are worried it is making us overweight and unhealthy.

So, what can you do? Lots of things! Everyone in the family can participate in healthy activities and eat a healthy, low-fat diet.

Some Simple Rules

Here are some simple rules to get you on the road to better health. First, think about nutrition. Are you eating a variety of good foods or mostly snacks and junk foods with lots of sugar or fat? There's one good way to tell. Learn to read the food labels. Pick two kinds of cereal for example. Read the label on the side of each box and compare calories, fats, sugars, and carbohydrates.

Also, think about how much you eat. Compared to other people in the world, Americans eat giant portions. Did you know that one serving of meat should be about the size of your palm? One serving of spaghetti, rice, or pasta is only the size of a baseball. How big is the serving of spaghetti you get at your favorite Italian restaurant? One way to start eating healthier is to put smaller portions on your plate—you can even use a smaller plate! Also, eat more slowly. Did you know it takes 20 minutes for your stomach to tell your brain that you are full? Eating two or three huge meals a day is bad for your body. It is better to eat several small meals throughout the day. Most doctors agree that you should eat four to five small meals of good, nutritious foods each day.

Is exercise really that important? Absolutely, say weight specialists. Not only is exercise good for people who want to lose weight, it is good for everyone. Exercise, like walking each day for just 10–15 minutes, makes your heart stronger. If you sit at a desk working all day, it's good to get up and stretch your muscles. It helps burn calories so you can lose weight. One pound of fat (think of a pound of butter) is worth 3,500 calories. That means if you want to lose one pound a week, you must eat 3,500 fewer calories that week. This means cutting down 500 calories each day. Or, eat less and exercise more.

You can get more exercise in a variety of ways, like washing the car or raking leaves. Walking burns calories, and the faster you walk the more calories you burn. Think about all the things you do in a day. Where can you build in a few extra steps? Walk to the store. Take the stairs instead of using the elevator. Turn off the TV and computer and get moving!

Here are some other healthy eating tips.

- Fat-free or "lite" foods often have added sugar and salt. In fact, researchers have found that drinking diet soda can actually make you gain—not lose—weight! Look for foods that are naturally low in fat and calories, like fruit. Try water with lemon instead of diet soda.

- Pack your own lunch so you aren't tempted to eat out. Many quick restaurant lunch choices are packed with fat and calories. It's hard to make a healthy selection when you're in a hurry. It's better to plan ahead and prepare a healthy lunch at home.

- When you compare labels, look at the serving size. The number of calories listed will be for one serving. A small snack package often contains more than one serving. It's better to measure out and pack your own snacks so that you are in control of what you're eating.

- Doctors also say that skipping meals is a very bad idea. In fact, it can slow your metabolism down enough to make you gain weight. Don't go more

than a couple of hours without a healthy meal or snack. That will keep your energy up and make it less likely that you will get so hungry that you grab a candy bar or doughnut.

Just thinking about your health is not enough. Make smart, healthy choices every day to feel better. Talk to everyone in your family. Discuss what choices are hurting, or not helping, your health. Make a plan to change. Ask each person in your family for ideas. Practice reading labels and comparing servings and calories. Take turns packing lunches. Set goals to eat more fruits and vegetables and to eat smaller portions. Plan healthy family meals and fun family outings. Together, you can all make good choices for a healthier family life!

1 About the Reading. Choose the answer that best completes the statement and write it on the line.

1. Americans are lucky to have a _____ of food in their diets.
   a. serving   b. value   c. portion   d. variety

2. Millions of Americans have a serious weight problem known as _____.
   a. metabolism   b. disease   c. obesity   d. diabetes

3. The way we buy food and eat has changed a lot now that we have _____ and
   _____.
   a. stoves and microwaves   c. milkmen and fish markets
   b. grocery stores and refrigerators   d. gardens and bakeries

4. Doctors say you should eat 4 or 5 _____ each day.
   a. TV dinners   b. healthy snacks   c. large meals   d. small meals

5. The _____ size we get in restaurants is usually more than we should eat.
   a. serving   b. pasta   c. calories   d. nutrition

6. Good _____ is the proper balance of proteins, carbohydrates, fats, and sugar.
   a. health   b. nutrition   c. metabolism   d. cholesterol

7. Food labels list the nutrients by _____ size.
   a. pound   b. person   c. plate   d. portion

8. Your _____ can slow down and make you gain weight if you skip meals.
   a. disease   b. nutrition   c. metabolism   d. calories

9. If you want to buy healthier food, learning how to read _____ is the first step.
   a. labors   b. ladles   c. ladders   d. labels

10. Exercise does more than just help you lose weight; it also makes your _____
    stronger.
    a. heart   b. heard   c. heat   d. head

11. If you are an unhealthy weight, you may be at risk for getting _____.
    a. high blood pressure   b. high cholesterol   c. diabetes   d. a, b, and c

12. The best lunch is one you _____ yourself.
    a. prevent   b. preview   c. prepare   d. prescribe

What do you think? Do you know someone who needs to lose weight and become healthier? What could you tell that person (maybe it's you!) that might help him or her to make smarter choices? Be sure to include reasons that explain your answer.

_____

_____

_____

_____

How can parents set a good example for being healthy? Name three things parents can do to help their children lead healthier lives.

_____

_____

_____

_____

2 Which Word Does Not Fit? Choose the word in each row that does *not* have the same meaning as the other words, and write it on the line. Study the example before you begin.

1. grocery store	market	bakery	food store	**bakery**
2. chain	super	great	huge	_____
3. tag	sticker	label	list	_____
4. obese	diseased	fat	overweight	_____
5. starving	drinking	hungry	empty	_____
6. type	thing	kind	sort	_____
7. specialist	nurse	expert	master	_____
8. portion	diet	slice	serving	_____
9. mild	serious	dangerous	grave	_____
10. scientist	expert	dentist	researcher	_____
11. actually	truly	really	likely	_____
12. choice	decision	question	selection	_____

3 Spelling. Change the *y* to *i,* and then add -*ness* to these words. Study the example before you begin.

1. sleepy _____sleepiness_____

2. ugly _____

3. dizzy _____

4. healthy _____

5. nasty _____

6. lovely _____

7. dusty _____

8. greasy _____

9. holy _____

10. fruity _____

4 Reading a Nutrition Label. Nutrition labels can help you shop, plan meals, and prepare healthy foods every day. A nutritious diet includes lots of fruits and vegetables, whole grains, low-fat dairy products, lean meats and poultry, fish, beans, and nuts. Read the nutrition labels below. Use them to help you answer the questions which follow.

Fruit & Nut Oat Bar

Nutrition Facts		
Serving Size 1 bar		
Servings per container 1		% Daily
Calories 135		Value
Total Fat	5.2g	8%
Saturated fat	1.0g	5%
Trans fat	0mg	
Cholesterol	0mg	0%
Sodium	71mg	3%
Total Carbohydrate	17.8g	6%
Dietary Fiber	5.3g	21%
Sugars	2.3g	
Protein	2.2g	
Calcium	36mg	
Potassium	238mg	
Vitamin D		15%

Honey-Nut Raisin Bar

Nutrition Facts		
Serving Size 1 bar		
Servings per container 1		% Daily
Calories 402		Value
Total Fat	6.8g	11%
Saturated fat	2.7g	13%
Trans fat	4mg	
Cholesterol	0mg	0%
Sodium	253mg	10%
Total Carbohydrate	77.4g	26%
Dietary Fiber	3.6g	6%
Sugars	47.9g	
Protein	7.1g	
Calcium	19.3mg	
Potassium	109.8mg	

1. How many calories will you consume if you eat 2 Fruit & Nut Oat Bars?

_____

_____

2. If you are watching your cholesterol and fat intake, which bar is the healthier choice? Why?

_____

_____

3. Trans fats can increase your risk of heart disease. Which bar is the best choice for your heart?

_____

_____

4. If you were on a 10k bike ride and needed protein for energy, which bar would you choose?

_____

_____

5. Excess sodium can increase your risk of high blood pressure. If you are worried about your blood pressure, which bar is better for you?

_____

_____

6. Fiber and sugars are types of carbohydrates. Whole grains supply healthy carbs that give your body fiber and long-lasting energy. Sugars are high in calories and low in nutrients. Your body gets only short bursts of energy from sugary carbs. Which bar supplies the healthiest carbohydrates?

_____

_____

7. If you were looking for a low-calorie, low-fat snack, which bar would you choose? Why?

_____

_____

8. Who should eat the bar you did not choose? Why?

_____

_____

5 Words That End with -ness. To complete these sentences correctly, choose the best word from the list and add -ness to it. Study the example before you begin.

aware	eager	forgetful	good	loud	serious
calm	✓fond	forgive	graceful	rude	still

1. Since her childhood, Chris had had a ___**fondness**___ for candy bars, but she has learned to limit herself to just one a week.

2. When the _____ of the car radio made Andrew's ears throb with pain, he asked his friend if he could turn it down.

3. "Do not let the _____ of a few diners keep you from treating everyone politely," the manager told the new waiter who was disappointed that he didn't get a tip.

4. The shopper quickly begged the woman's _____ after he almost tripped her while rushing down the bakery aisle to grab the last loaf of rye bread.

5. The _____ of the dancers in the musical inspired Nancy to sign up for a dance class during her lunch hour.

6. A restaurant's success often depends on the chef's _____ of the likes and dislikes of the local diners.

7. In his _____ to get to work early, Carl foolishly left his wallet on the kitchen counter at his mother-in-law's apartment and was unable to get on the subway.

8. As if in a trance, the family sat in complete _____ after eating a huge meal of spaghetti and meatballs and Italian bread.

9. The ad for the new yogurt-coated oat cereal raved about its _____ and even stated that it was a complete, nutritious meal.

10. Aunt Joyce's _____ was getting so bad that even when her nieces and nephews showed up at her doorstep, she had nothing to feed them and didn't even remember inviting them over for dinner.

11. When Amrita gets home from yoga class, she always has a cup of herbal tea so she can enjoy the feeling of _____.

12. When the waitress asked the small boy what he would like for dinner, with all _____ he said, "ice cream."

Words for Study

previous	traditional	Pilgrims	ethnicity
amber	medley	population	diverse
fascinated	unusual	community	diversity
dimples	portrait	traditions	ethnic
introduced	immigrants	bureau	continent

LESSON 2
An American Family Portrait

A guest at a wedding saw a cute little boy across the room. His name was Benjamin. He was the groom's son from a previous marriage. Benjamin was dressed up, wearing a smart suit and tie. He had straight, shiny, dark brown hair. His skin was the color of amber honey. However, the guest was fascinated by Benjamin's dimples on both cheeks. When the boy laughed, his dimples would show. The guest came up to him. She bent down and said, "My goodness, where did you get those charming dimples?"

She heard a voice behind her. "From his grandmother, of course!" The little boy turned around. He gave a very pale-skinned, blonde lady a hug. Then Benjamin said in German, "Ya, mein uma!" He spoke English next. "That means from my grandma!" He ran off to play with the other children.

The grandmother smiled. She had dimples too. She was very tiny, and had bright blue eyes. The guest was embarrassed. She tried to explain. "I'm sorry, he's so . . . so *dark,* and you're so . . . so *light!*" she said with a red face.

The grandmother laughed. "That's okay," she replied. "This is how the new American family *really* looks."

Her name was Inge, she said. The guest asked Inge to tell her family story.

Inge said she was born in Germany. She married Richard, a U.S. soldier working in her German hometown. He was an African American from Virginia. He was handsome with very dark skin, she said. Later, they moved back to Virginia. Inge and her husband had two children. Inge said they were born with golden skin and green eyes. Inge pointed to her grown-up son, the groom. His skin was the same color as Benjamin's, but he had brown curly hair. "When he was a child, he had curly blonde hair!" she laughed. Then, Inge introduced the guest to another older lady. She wore a traditional satin,

Japanese gown. She bowed. She was Japanese, and she was the mother of the bride.

Later the family gathered for the photographer. They were going to take a group picture. Everyone was laughing and chattering. It was a medley of people of different colors speaking many languages. "Please hold still," the photographer said. Then, she snapped the picture.

Long ago this might have been an unusual American family portrait. But not these days. Ever since the early 1600s, people from other countries have been coming here. They are called *immigrants*. Years ago, people used to ask, "Where are you from?" Back then, most Americans, other than Native Americans, were from somewhere else.

Starting with the Jamestown Settlement in 1607 and the English Pilgrims in 1620, people have come to settle in America. In the middle of the 1800s many German and Irish came. Their crops failed at home, and there was nothing to eat. They came to America to start over. Africans were brought as slaves to work. They did not want to leave Africa, but were forced to come. Later, other people from Denmark, Holland, Sweden, Spain, Italy, Romania, and Hungary came too. These early immigrants were just the first of many to leave their homelands and head for America.

Today people from all over the world are still coming to America. They come from Ethiopia, Nigeria, or Ghana. Or maybe from India, Vietnam, Nicaragua, Mexico, China, or Russia. Immigrants go to towns where friends or relatives live. San Francisco's population is one-third Asian American. California's population is 36% Hispanic and Latino. California, Texas, Florida, and New York have the largest numbers of immigrants.

When new people arrive, they join the community. They meet people at schools, churches, and work.

With new friends, they get married and make a new family picture. Their children will grow up learning different traditions. Many will speak two or more languages. One recent study found that the U.S. has nearly 35 million Spanish speakers.

The U.S. Census Bureau collects information about the race and ethnicity of Americans. Every 10 years the Census Bureau counts how many people live in the U.S. It asks about how people live—where they live and who lives with them. It also records what kinds of jobs we do. It knows how many farmers, nurses, and teachers there are.

The census bureau says our population is more diverse than ever before. This means there are many more families like Inge's. She has African American, Japanese, German, and Swedish people all in one family. Do you wonder why is there more diversity today? It is because new immigrants are coming from different places.

But how would Inge's family answer the census questions about ethnicity? In the past the census has forced people to choose one race or ethnicity. The word *other* is not a good choice either. The 2010 census will allow people to choose more than one race. A person can check White, African American, and Japanese. Some experts believe putting a label on a person is not the best idea. But others explain why it is important. A manager at a health clinic gives her reason.

"If we know someone's ethnic background, we can help them with special problems," she said. "Older Hispanic people, for example, may have diabetes and might not speak English. We must find where they live. Then, we can send a notice to them. They can come in for a free diabetes test or get medicine," she says.

Our families in America look different than they did years ago. New faces and new languages are everywhere. Today your neighbor may have a Kenyan mother and a Chinese father. Their children might speak English, Chinese, and Kiswahili. There will be more families like this in the future. We will all have interesting things to share. Who does the new American family look like? Everyone!

1 About the Reading. Answer the following questions in good sentence form.

1. Why was the wedding guest surprised to see Benjamin with his grandmother?

_____

_____

2. How do you think Benjamin would describe his family?

_____

_____

3. Inge was born in one country, and then she married a man from another country and moved there. Have you lived in another country? Which country or countries have you lived in?

_____

_____

4. What is the job of the U.S. Census Bureau?

_____

_____

5. Name three states that have large immigrant populations. Why do you think immigrants go to these places?

_____

_____

6. How do you describe your own ethnicity? Do you think it's important to know the ethnicity of people in the U.S.?

_____

_____

7. Describe your own family. What countries are your family members from? What races are included in your family?

_____

_____

_____

_____

8. Have you ever been in a situation where you were surprised to find out that people of different races were in the same family? How did you respond? How would you respond if you were the wedding guest?

_____

_____

_____

_____

2 Where Do They Come From? Match the people to the country or continent from which they come.

Africans	Cubans	Germans	Koreans	Pacific Islanders
Americans	Dutch	Greeks	Mexicans	Romanians
Asians	Egyptians	Hungarians	Nicaraguans	Russians
Canadians	English	Irish	Nigerians	Swedes
Chinese	French	Japanese	Norwegians	Swiss

_____ 1. Africa

_____ 2. America

_____ 3. Asia

_____ 4. Canada

_____ 5. China

_____ 6. Cuba

_____ 7. Egypt

_____ 8. England

_____ 9. France

_____ 10. Germany

_____ 11. Greece

_____ 12. Holland

_____ 13. Hungary

_____ 14. Ireland

_____ 15. Japan

_____ 16. Korea

_____ 17. Mexico

_____ 18. Nicaragua

_____ 19. Nigeria

_____ 20. Norway

_____ 21. Pacific Islands

_____ 22. Romania

_____ 23. Russia

_____ 24. Sweden

_____ 25. Switzerland

3 Words That End with -*ment*. To complete these sentences correctly, choose the best word from the list and add -*ment* to it. Study the example before you begin.

advance	commit	discourage	engage	enlarge	measure
ail	confine	encourage	enjoy	manage	✓ship

1. When the clerk informed him that the __**shipment**__ of fresh lettuce wasn't expected until next Tuesday, Uncle Adolf was annoyed.

2. Hassan ordered an _____ of his girlfriend's photograph for his desk at work.

3. When thirty-year-old Gail shyly produced the _____ ring Ray had given her, her mother burst out, "But you're too young to be thinking about marriage!"

4. Bobby was unable to complete the _____ exercise his math teacher had given for homework because he had lost his ruler.

5. Holly declared she would make a _____ to stop smoking if her husband, in turn, would agree to lose forty-five pounds.

6. After describing the symptoms of his _____, Walter was surprised when Dr. Stern remarked calmly, "My dear fellow, your problem is not physical; it's emotional."

7. The sign in the hotel lobby read, "The _____ hopes you will enjoy your stay in Los Angeles."

8. Ms. Bond suddenly found little _____ in cooking now that everyone in her family was on a strict low-fat diet.

9. Because of the many opportunities for _____, Martha chose a career in sales.

10. Most of us need a little _____ to put more effort into reaching our goals.

11. In spite of receiving many words of _____ from his relatives, Charles decided to risk going into business for himself.

12. During his _____ in prison, John learned that although he was surrounded by people, he was very much alone.

4 The Capitol and Capitals. The Capitol is the building in Washington, D.C., where the Congress of the United States meets. Each state has a capitol where the state government meets. The capitals listed below are cities that are the seats of government for the states in which they are located. Use a map of the United States or a dictionary to match these capitals with their states.

Austin	Denver	Nashville	Springfield
Boston	Honolulu	Oklahoma City	Tallahassee
Columbia	Jackson	Sacramento	Topeka
Columbus	Lansing	Salt Lake City	Trenton

1. The capital of California is _____.

2. The capital of Colorado is _____.

3. The capital of Florida is _____.

4. The capital of Hawaii is _____.

5. The capital of Illinois is _____.

6. The capital of Kansas is _____.

7. The capital of Massachusetts is _____.

8. The capital of Michigan is _____.

9. The capital of Mississippi is _____.

10. The capital of New Jersey is _____.

11. The capital of Ohio is _____.

12. The capital of Oklahoma is _____.

13. The capital of South Carolina is _____.

14. The capital of Tennessee is _____.

15. The capital of Texas is _____.

16. The capital of Utah is _____.

Words for Study

multiples	biologists	separate	substitute	unique
celebrities	science	fertility	organization	personality
quintuplets	abilities	especially	individuals	similarity
superstitious	fraternal	pediatricians	challenging	gymnastics

LESSON 3
Life with Multiples

You've seen them at the store or maybe in the park. Those baby strollers with room for two, even three, babies. Twins, triplets, and multiples of any kind always get a lot of attention. When moms give birth to four, or more children, it usually makes the news. The families are often treated like celebrities. One such case was the famous 1934 Dionne Quintuplets of Canada. That was the first recorded birth of five children at the same time that all survived. In the U.S. in 1997, Bobbi and Kenny McCaughey became famous parents when a record seven babies were born to them. And in January 2009, Nadya Suleman of California gave birth to the longest living octuplets in the U.S.— so far.

We seem to be fascinated with twins and multiples. But do you know that some people are afraid of twins? Some cultures believe that twins are good luck. Others believe that they are a sign of bad luck. Superstitious beliefs about twins have persisted for centuries. Some people do not understand how or why twins or multiples could happen. And they believe it is a mistake of nature, since it is so rare.

Since biologists discovered the science of twins and multiples, it is no longer a mystery. Researchers learned that *identical* twins come from one egg being split into two embryos. When the babies are born, they have the same gene information. Genes are the message carriers in cells that determine hair and skin color, height, and the way a person looks. Some also believe genes pass on special abilities from parents, like a knack for music or art. Sometimes, identical twins look so much alike you can't tell them apart. Even parents have trouble!

But not all twins are identical. Babies born at the same time that do not look alike are called *fraternal twins*. They are created when two separate eggs form into embryos at the same time. Very often fraternal twins don't look anything like each other because they do not share exactly the same genes. Embryos can be formed by three, four, or more eggs at the

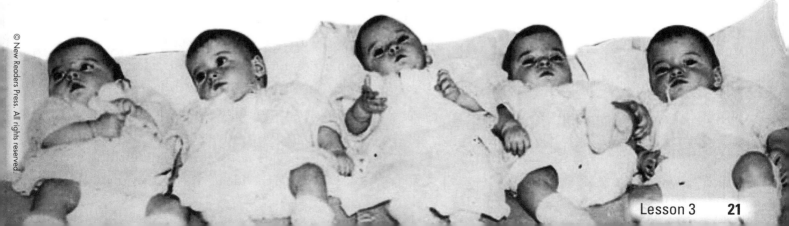

same time. Three embryos become triplets. Four become quadruplets. And five become quintuplets.

The overall rate of multiple births has been increasing. Scientists believe the increase is caused mainly by two factors: women are giving birth at an older age and more women are using fertility drugs. The chances of having a multiple birth already increase with a woman's age, but when you add to that the advancements in fertility treatments, you get a multiple baby boom. In 1990 there were 13 sets of quintuplets born. But in 2006 there were 67 sets of quints born.

In general, the chances of giving birth to twins in the 21st century are about 3%. That's more than double what the odds were just 25 years ago. If twins run in your family, that increases your odds as well. In 2000, Jon and Kate Gosselin of Pennsylvania had twin girls with the help of fertility treatments. Just four years later, Kate gave birth to sextuplets—that's six babies at once! Soon all 10 Gosselins were the stars of a popular cable TV show.

Having twins or multiples is a lot of work. One mom from Baltimore, named Cathy, described her experiences. "When the doctor said I was having twins, I cried and cried. I was happy and excited, but I was also so worried! I already had one older girl, Ellen, who was four. I knew how much work and attention one baby needed, so, all I could think of was, how can I do twice as much?"

Aliyah, another mom from Ohio, said when her twins were born, they got a lot of attention.

"Everywhere I went, people would stop and look at the babies. They would say, 'How cute! It must be fun to have twins.'" Aliyah said she would smile and say thank you. But she always introduced her son Devon, who was six at the time. "Devon didn't get much attention anymore. I didn't want him to feel left out. It is important that *all* my children feel special, not just the twins."

Both Aliyah and Cathy said people who don't have multiples have no idea about the work involved, especially when the children are young. "It's a lot of work. It takes all day to take care of them. They always need something. I am always tired," said Aliyah. She said most people think feeding or changing diapers is just doing the same thing two or three times. But parents with multiples say it is not at all like this. Their days can be crazy.

Pediatricians say parents must be in control of the situation. They must decide which ways of coping with their multiples will work best. The parents must take care of each child's needs and wants. If there are other children in the family, they can help out as well. But doctors also caution parents to be careful, and not let siblings become substitute parents.

Having multiples is expensive. Parents need two or three—or more—of everything. Three high chairs and three sets of clothes and socks and shoes. Diapers for three, plus cribs and toys. Car seats and baby bottles and baby food—all multiplied by three. Parents agree that it is very stressful, but it is also very exciting!

A mom with her own twins started one organization for parents of twins. Her name is Pamela, and she offers advice for parents on raising twins and other multiples. Pamela says that the early years are the most challenging. "When they are young, they do not seem very different. It's hard to see them as individuals. But as they grow up, it is exciting to watch each one develop his or her own unique personality."

Now Cathy's twins are nine years old, and they are very different. One of her twins likes music and reading, and the other likes sports and artwork. "Just because they look the same, I can tell you that is where the similarity ends," Cathy explains. She was surprised to find out how different the twins are becoming as they grow up. She describes one as a little lazy about doing homework, but very creative with painting and drawing. The other one is an excellent student, and loves gymnastics and other sports. "They are together here with me and I do the same thing for both of them, and yet they are turning out very different. It is very surprising," Cathy says.

1 About the Reading. Put the letter of the correct answer on the line.

1. Quintuplets are _____ children born at the same time.
   a. two　　　　　**b.** three　　　　　**c.** four　　　　　**d.** five

2. The Dionne Quintuplets were born in _____.
   a. the U.S.　　　**b.** Canada　　　　**c.** Germany　　　**d.** California

3. Families of multiples are often treated like _____.
   a. celebrities　　**b.** centuries　　　**c.** cellars　　　　**d.** cereals

4. People who are superstitious might be _____ of twins.
   a. proud　　　　**b.** frightened　　　**c.** embarrassed　　**d.** panicky

5. Two babies born together that are not exactly alike are known as _____.
   a. identical twins　**b.** fraternal multiples　**c.** fraternal twins　**d.** fraternal triplets

6. If a set of twins contains a boy and a girl, then they are _____.
   a. identical twins　**b.** fraternal multiples　**c.** fraternal twins　**d.** fraternal triplets

7. The rising rate of multiple births is probably caused by _____.
   a. younger mothers and the use of fertility treatments
   b. older mothers and the use of fertility treatments
   c. fertility treatments and advancements in drugs
   d. women giving birth more often and fertility drugs

8. The chance of giving birth to twins is about _____.
   a. once every three births　　　**c.** three in one thousand births
   b. three in ten births　　　　　**d.** three in one hundred births

9. If having twins is twice the work of having one baby, then having triplets is _____.
   a. three times the work　　　　**c.** five times the work
   b. four times the work　　　　　**d.** hardly any work at all

10. Pediatricians are _____.

    a. doctors who specialize in siblings   **c.** doctors who care for babies and children

    b. doctors who care for mothers   **d.** doctors who specialize in multiples

11. If a car seat costs $125 and a crib costs $490, you would spend _____ on car seats and cribs for quintuplets.

    a. $2,460   **b.** $1,845   **c.** $2,975   **d.** $3,075

12. Even though multiples can be _____ in many ways, they usually have _____ personalities.

    a. unique, likeable   **b.** similar, unique   **c.** similar, challenging   **d.** separate, similar

2 Synonyms. A *synonym* is a word that has almost the same meaning as another word. Match each word with its synonym. Study the example before you begin.

ability	advancement	diverse	obese	✓similar	substitute
absolute	convenient	individual	separate	specialist	unique

___similar___   **1.** alike   _____   **7.** person

_____   **2.** expert   _____   **8.** replace

_____   **3.** handy   _____   **9.** skill

_____   **4.** improvement   _____   **10.** split

_____   **5.** one of a kind   _____   **11.** total

_____   **6.** overweight   _____   **12.** varied

3 Antonyms. An *antonym* is a word whose meaning is nearly opposite to the meaning of another word. Match each word with its antonym. Study the example before you begin.

challenging	convenient	diverse	multiple	✓separate	supersized
confinement	discouragement	fertile	obese	specialize	unusual

___separate___   **1.** connect   _____   **7.** infertile

_____   **2.** easy   _____   **8.** regular

_____   **3.** encouragement   _____   **9.** single

_____   **4.** freedom   _____   **10.** similar

_____   **5.** generalize   _____   **11.** thin

_____   **6.** inconvenient   _____   **12.** tiny

4 Spelling. To form the plural of these words which end in *f* or *fe*, you must first change the *f* to *v*. Then, if the word already ends in *e*, add only *s*; otherwise add *–es*. Study the examples before you begin.

1. thief   **thieves**   6. loaf _____

2. calf _____   7. shelf _____

3. elf _____   8. self _____

4. half _____   9. wife   **wives** _____

5. leaf _____   10. knife _____

5 Capitalization Rules: Part 1. In order to capitalize words correctly, you need to know certain rules. Study the rules below. Then capitalize the words in the sentences that follow. The number at the end of each sentence tells you how many words need to be capitalized in that sentence. Study the example before you begin.

1. **Capitalize the first letter of the first word in a sentence.**

   Example: The more John read of the book, the more he enjoyed it.

2. **Capitalize people's names.**

   Example: Last night Mrs. Harvey visited Aunt Elizabeth.

3. **Capitalize the word *I*.**

   Example: After watching the late movie on television, I fell asleep.

4. **Capitalize calendar items.**

   Examples: days of the week .... Thursday, Saturday

              months of the year .... January, April

              holidays and holy days .... Valentine's Day, Easter

   Note: Do not capitalize seasons.

   Example: Of all the seasons of the year, I like spring the best.

5. **Capitalize place names.**

   Examples: parts of the world .... Europe, the Middle East, the North Pole

              countries and sections of a country ..... Egypt, Canada, New England, the Great Plains

              states and provinces .... Oklahoma, Illinois, Ontario

              counties .... Stuart County

              cities and towns .... Seattle, Jamestown

streets	Main Street, Penny Lane
islands	Hawaiian Islands, Bear Island
mountains	Rocky Mountains, Mount Washington
bodies of water	Gulf of Mexico, Great Salt Lake, the Nile River, the Black Sea
structures and public places	the White House, Central Park, the Golden Gate Bridge, the Statue of Liberty

Note: Do not capitalize *the* when it appears before a name.

1. John and Mary had their first serious argument when he wanted to go to Cape Cod for their honeymoon and she wanted to go to the Thousand Islands. (6)

2. on the fourth of july, people crowded along the banks of the ohio river to watch the fireworks display. (5)

3. roger had been to south america and africa many times on business trips, but he had not yet visited any of the countries in europe. (5)

4. mrs. price always started her christmas shopping in late october and had all her packages mailed by thanksgiving. (5)

5. on good friday, dr. lodge and her children attended the worship service at the church on chestnut street. (7)

6. when kate moved from her cramped apartment near carver city hospital to a huge estate on riverside lane, she felt as if she had entered heaven. (7)

7. ruth slipped the book about andrew jackson into her handbag so she would have something interesting to read during her flight to england on monday. (5)

8. buddy couldn't wait until august when he would be camping in the great smoky mountains for three weeks with dr. carpenter and his family. (7)

9. mr. knight couldn't recall the number of his niece's home, so he just wrote rosebud lane, columbia, south carolina, on the envelope and hoped the letter would get there. (7)

10. "i think i will spend the winter in honolulu before i visit you in vermont," said uncle steven, who had never enjoyed cold weather. (7)

Words for Study

scenery	elaborate	vivid	memory
irritation	costumes	polka-dot	prescription
imagine	shuffled	fabulous	immune
immediately	anxiety	behavior	interrupted
theatrical	exotic	Alzheimer's	hereditary

LESSON 4
Lunch with Grandma Janey

Lisa sat slumped in the front seat of the car, with her head against the window. She barely noticed the passing scenery of the bright spring day. Every week it was the same thing. Lisa would help her mom, Marcia, who was Grandma's daughter, fix a nice lunch. After a few bites, Grandma Janey would start complaining about the food. Or, sometimes Grandma forgot where she was. Oh, why did people have to get old! Lisa thought to herself with irritation.

Suddenly, she felt a small wave of guilt. What if her own mother came down with the same disease! What if someday it would be her turn to cook a lunch that went uneaten! She couldn't imagine her own mother acting the way Grandma Janey often did.

The car pulled into the driveway of Grandma Janey's old house. Lisa and her mom walked in through the old screened-in porch. It was covered by masses of flowering pink roses. "Grandma Janey, we're here," Marcia called out cheerily as the door banged behind them. The place was dark as usual. Immediately Lisa and her mother pulled open the drapes. Sunlight gleamed off the glass-framed displays of theatrical photos. They showed pictures of a young woman posing, wearing all kinds of elaborate costumes.

With her wooden cane assisting her, Grandma Janey shuffled into the room.

"Hello, Marcia, dear, and you too, Lisa, such a nice day! Did you see all the roses out front?" she said with a broad smile.

Lisa smiled back and reached up to hug

the older woman. Despite her anxiety, Lisa truly loved Grandma Janey, especially the exotic way she looked and dressed. Today, a jeweled clip held back her vivid red hair. She had shiny orange lipstick, sky blue eye shadow, and dark penciled eyebrows. Lime green slacks matched her flowered blouse and red belt, and long polka-dot neck scarf. A necklace of blue cut-glass beads sparkled in the sunlight.

"This is a pretty flashy outfit, Grandma Janey!" Lisa said brightly.

"Too many people forget how to dress properly these days," Grandma Janey said with a frown. Then she banged the floor with her cane to be sure she made her point.

"Why, when I was on stage," she began, and then looked out into space without finishing the sentence. But Lisa already knew the story. Years ago, Grandma Janey had been a famous theatrical star called the "Fabulous Jeannine." As she grew older, the actress started forgetting her lines and acting confused. Some people thought her grandmother's behavior was caused by a drinking problem. But it was something called Alzheimer's disease.

At the school library, Lisa had read more about it. More than a hundred years ago, a German doctor studied people who had memory problems. This doctor discovered that people had a real disease that affected nerve cells. Since his name was Alzheimer, the disease he discovered was called Alzheimer's disease.

Today, the lunch went better than usual, with Grandma Janey not complaining too much. Afterwards, Lisa and her mom stopped at the drugstore for Grandma Janey's prescription. Lisa looked at all the medical brochures near the counter. Many of them had pictures of older people.

"Mom, why do old people get all these diseases? I thought it was kids that were always sick?" she asked.

Marcia frowned while thinking of the answer. "Well, kids get sick, but they get well fast. When you get older, your immune system isn't as strong and . . ."

"But what's an immune system?" Lisa interrupted.

"Oh, that's what protects your body from illness. It's like an army of soldiers ready to fight off disease. Older people like Grandma don't have as many soldiers as somebody your age." Marcia pointed to the medical brochures. They had information on heart disease, high cholesterol, diabetes, and other conditions.

"These are all chronic conditions. A chronic condition is something you have for a long time. Most people over age 60 have at least one or two of them."

"Are you going to have all these problems when you get old?" asked Lisa.

Marcia gave her daughter a reassuring squeeze around her shoulder. "Let's not worry now. Besides, there are medicines people can take so they can live pretty normal lives," Marcia replied, calmly.

As they got into the car with the prescription, Lisa thought hard about being an older person. What would it be like to have to take pills every day she wondered? She turned to her mother.

"Mom, this Alzheimer's thing, what if *you* get that disease? Or, some of those other diseases! Will I have to take care of you, and . . ." Lisa's voice trailed off and her eyes were wide in alarm.

Marcia turned and smiled at her daughter. "Nobody can predict the future, Lisa. Scientists are studying these chronic diseases every day for answers. And Grandma Janey's doctors said now there's a new memory test. This test can predict the chances of getting Alzheimer's. It's only hereditary in a small number of people. Anyway, I take pretty good care of myself. Maybe when you are Grandma's age, there won't even be as many illnesses. And besides, I'm not nearly the picky eater she is!"

Lisa nodded her head; then she started to giggle. "Maybe there won't be diseases, but who is going to cure people from wearing crazy outfits!"

They both laughed as they drove up Grandma Janey's street.

1 About the Story. Answer the following questions in good sentence form.

1. What kind of mood was Lisa in at the beginning of the story?

_____

2. How does Lisa's mood change when she gets to Grandma Janey's house? Explain why her mood changes.

_____

_____

3. What is Grandma Janey's house like?

_____

4. Why do you think Grandma Janey dresses the way she does?

_____

5. What do you know about Alzheimer's disease? Do you know anyone who has Alzheimer's disease or memory problems?

_____

_____

_____

6. What is your immune system? What kinds of things can cause your immune system to fail?

_____

_____

_____

7. What chronic conditions do you know about? Do you or does someone you know have a chronic condition? Explain.

_____

_____

_____

8. At the end of the story, we find out what Lisa is really worried about. What is it?

_____

9. What would you say to Lisa if she were your daughter?

_____

_____

10. What do you worry about as you or a loved one gets older? Are there any hereditary diseases in your family?

_____

_____

_____

2 Synonyms. Match each word with its synonym.

anxiety	behavior	elaborate	fabulous	medley	scenery
assist	costume	exotic	immune	previously	theater

_____ **1.** unusual

_____ **2.** wonderful

_____ **3.** safe

_____ **4.** actions

_____ **5.** help

_____ **6.** stage

_____ **7.** before

_____ **8.** mixture

_____ **9.** nervousness

_____ **10.** outfit

_____ **11.** complex

_____ **12.** view

3 Antonyms. Match each word with its antonym.

advance	elaborate	forget	picky	uneaten	usual
broad	flashy	irritate	slump	unknown	vivid

_____ **1.** plain

_____ **2.** unusual

_____ **3.** consumed

_____ **4.** soothe

_____ **5.** retreat

_____ **6.** simple

_____ **7.** narrow

_____ **8.** remember

_____ **9.** easy to please

_____ **10.** straighten

_____ **11.** famous

_____ **12.** pale

4 More Work with the Ending -ness. To complete these sentences correctly, choose the best word from the list and add -ness to it.

bitter	dull	gentle	polite	stiff
dry	fresh	plump	smooth	truthful

1. The _____ of the fruits and vegetables at the farmer's market drew customers from all over town.

2. The _____ of the well-mannered children who were collecting money to fight world hunger so impressed Mr. Bergman that he gave them fifty dollars.

3. Mrs. Darling enjoyed being able to feel the _____ of her husband's skin after he completely shaved off his beard.

4. Ever since Ben's automobile accident, the _____ in his left shoulder told him when it was going to rain.

5. The _____ of the movie caused Miguel to fall fast asleep in the theater.

6. After the doctor told him that the _____ of Arizona's climate would greatly improve his health, Jesse decided to consider moving there.

7. Staring uneasily at her _____ in the mirror, Sue realized that she had to do something about her weight, which meant starting a strict diet—tomorrow.

8. "In all _____, Your Honor, I am not guilty of the charges brought against me," declared Van Porter, who had decided to defend himself instead of hiring a lawyer.

9. Rashid was filled with such _____ after suddenly being laid off that he vowed to go into business for himself so he'd never be treated like that again.

10. Ms. Harvey's voice always had a touch of _____ in it when she scolded students for not doing their homework, but they knew that she meant business.

5 Spelling. Change the *y* to *i* and add -ness. If necessary, review the examples in Lesson 1.

1. thirsty _____

2. risky _____

3. crazy _____

4. picky _____

5. noisy _____

6. nosy _____

7. bloody _____

8. flashy _____

9. scratchy _____

10. itchy _____

11. faulty _____

12. sneaky _____

6 Capitalization Rules: Part 2. Study the rules listed below. Then capitalize the words in the sentences that follow. Don't forget the rules you learned in Lesson 3. The number at the end of each sentence tells you how many letters need to be capitalized.

6. **Capitalize the names of races, nationalities, and languages.**

   Examples: races .... Native American, Asian, African American

   nationalities.................................... American, Canadian, French

   languages... English, French, Dutch

7. **Capitalize special events.**

   Examples: World Series, Washington County Fair

8. **Capitalize historical events and periods in history.**

   Examples: historical events .... Boston Tea Party, Battle of New Orleans

   periods in history .... Stone Age, World War II

9. **Capitalize the names of business firms and brand names of business products.**

   Examples: business firms.................................. Erie Shoe Company, National Bank of Los Angeles

   brand names.................................... Apple, Coke

10. **Capitalize the names of organizations.**

   Examples: government bodies .... the Congress, the State Department, the Georgia Supreme Court

   political organizations .... the Republican party

   institutions .... George Washington High School, Memphis State University

   associations .... Girl Scouts of America, the Cleveland Indians

1. when he was on the construction crew working on the new holiday inn, mr. holland always stopped at the greek diner on forest avenue for a cup of coffee and a muffin before going to work. (8)

2. adam bought two tickets to the super bowl game, hoping that the team he liked best—the dallas cowboys—would be playing in it. (5)

3. ms. woods couldn't find any books about the huron indians at the spring valley public library, so she chose one about the pueblo indians. (10)

4. when his ford stalled in front of bush county courthouse, louis realized he'd never make it to his appointment with the loan officer at standard savings and loan on time. (9)

5. the free ride insurance company paid dr. springfield $75,000 when the gas pedal on her brand-new rolls-royce stuck, and she drove through the window of roger's fish market on perch street. (14)

6. "i know this probably sounds like a phony excuse, mr. brooks," steven said nervously, "but my little brother dumped his glass of coke all over the report we're supposed to turn in tuesday on the war of 1812, and that's the honest truth." (7)

7. when the jackson family went to washington, d.c., they visited the capitol and met several members of congress. (7)

8. while tony lived with his aunt martha in springfield for six months, he went to falls road middle school. (9)

Words for Study

financial	practical	redecorate	imagination
debit	efficiently	furniture	appliances
credit	fluorescent	creative	consignment
minimum	bargain	clearance	purchase
depression	circulate	decorate	responsibly

LESSON 5

How to Spend Less and Have More Fun

Why are so many families in so much trouble?

Financial experts say that our use of debit and credit cards makes it easy to spend money we don't really have. You've probably heard stories like this one: A man buys a television for $350.00 on credit, but then makes only the minimum payment each month. If he's late with his payment, a fee is added. By the time he pays off the TV, it has cost him over $2000. Imagine what that extra $1650 could have paid for if he had planned better!

No one is immune to financial troubles, and these days families are being hit hard. In fact, the fastest growing part of the homeless population is families with children. In 2007, 23% of all homeless people were family members. And that doesn't count the families who have moved in with friends or extended family. Low-paying jobs and the high cost of housing are two of the biggest causes for this family crisis.

Debt is a tough problem to solve. It can quickly grow—even while you are trying to get rid of it. And people in debt suffer from stress, depression, and anxiety. They might even go out and buy things they don't need in order to make themselves feel better. That only makes the problem worse. But there are many ways to save money, and some of them are so simple you won't even feel the pinch. Let's look at some ways that families can enjoy life without letting their finances get out of control.

Tips to Keep Your Family out of Financial Trouble

Here are some practical ideas to help change your buying behavior. Sometimes, you might have to spend a little money to save a lot. However, before you do anything, get a notebook and write down everything you spend money on for two weeks— *everything*! You'll be surprised where your money goes. Then try these tips to cut down on your expenses.

Use what you have more efficiently. Look around the house. Did you know that just by turning off lights, TVs, or computers that you are not using, you could save money every month? About 5% of your monthly electric bill pays for devices that are turned off. You can also lower your bill by switching to energy-saving lightbulbs. The new compact fluorescent light (CFL) uses about a quarter of the electricity of an old bulb. It also lasts a lot longer.

Don't waste food. Many families try to save money by buying food in bulk and then freezing it. But without careful packaging, the food gets freezer burn and won't last. What a waste! If you want to make the most of the money you spend on food, invest in a food storage system. Then you can get together with friends or family to shop for bargains at a bulk food store. Divide and repackage the foods into useful portions in airtight freezer bags. Also, make sure your refrigerator and freezer are clean and neat so the cold air can circulate properly, protecting your investment.

Redecorate on a budget. If you're trying not to spend money on new things for your home, you might feel depressed looking at the same old furniture day after day. Instead of spending money you don't have on all new stuff, try giving your old furnishings a face-lift. First, look in magazines or go online to get some ideas. Then, get creative! Look for bargains on mis-mixed paint at the hardware store. Next, use clearance fabric or sheets from discount stores to cover old chairs and sofas. Frame your kids' artwork to decorate the walls. Even if money is tight, you don't have to be unhappy in your home. With a little money and a lot of imagination, you can have a cheerful space for the whole family to enjoy.

Sell unwanted items. Now, while you're redecorating, look in the closet, the basement, attic, and garage. Have your kids outgrown their toys? Do you have clothes, shoes, coats, books, or appliances you don't use anymore? If they are in good shape and still work, sell them! You can take them to a resale or consignment shop where someone else will sell them for you. Or, get some neighbors together and have a yard sale. You can even offer things for sale online. It takes some time and effort, but you can pay for your redecorating and maybe earn some extra money, too!

Say no to things you can't pay for. Try this trick to keep credit card spending under control. Put your cards in a bowl of water and put it in the freezer. Spend only cash. This is one way to freeze impulse buying. When you use credit to buy something on impulse, you don't think about how much you're spending or where the money will come from. Putting your credit cards on ice forces you to think about every purchase before you spend. Look at your debit and credit card bank statements every month. Make sure all the charges are correct. Look at everything you bought, and ask yourself if you really needed all those things. There might still be time to return a purchase if you have second thoughts.

Make a list before you shop. Buy only what is on the list, only what you have budgeted for. If your kids ask for extras, bargain with them. For example, tell them if they earn money to pay for half, you will pay the other half. Teach them about saving money and spending money responsibly. Open a savings account for each child, and set a good example for saving and checking statements.

Say yes to things you can do for free. Scan the local newspapers for free concerts, fairs, and special events. If your family enjoys movies, you can try the drive-in. You can usually get a good deal on taking a whole carload of kids to a drive-in movie. Some discount theaters offer a low price for movies that have been out for a while. And you could even get together with friends or neighbors to organize a DVD lending library. Sometimes you can find entertainment deals in newspapers or community newsletters, and other times you just have to be creative and come up with the ideas yourself.

Hold a family meeting. Everyone can talk about how they are willing to save money for things they want. You can discuss where you think spending is wasteful, and where you'd rather spend your money. You might be surprised to hear that your wife or husband and even your kids would rather save up toward a weekend trip than order pizza every weekend. Planning ahead can help your family spend money wisely and get the most enjoyment out of every penny.

1 About the Reading. Answer the following questions in good sentence form.

1. Name two reasons that many American families are homeless.

_____

2. What other factors might lead to a family being in a lot of debt?

_____

3. How do some people feel when they are in debt?

_____

4. Describe how you manage your own budget. Do you have debts? Do you have a plan for paying off your debts?

_____

_____

_____

5. What are some things people can do to lower the cost of electricity bills?

_____

_____

6. Name one way families can save money on food.

_____

7. What are some things families can do to make their homes look better without spending a lot of money?

_____

_____

8. What would happen if you put your credit cards in the freezer? Do you think it would help you spend less money?

_____

_____

9. What kinds of fun things do you and your family do for free or for very little money?

_____

_____

2 Word Families. Use the words in each set listed at the left to complete these sentences correctly.

decorator
decorations
redecorate

1. Elizabeth hired a _____ to _____ her apartment, but she didn't like the new _____ that were hung on the walls.

entertain
entertainment

2. Andrew looked in the _____ section of the newspaper to find something to _____ his nephews for the day.

capital
capitalize
capitalization

3. The teacher told us that we would have to use one hundred _____ letters in order to _____ every word correctly on the _____ test.

assist
assistant
assistance

4. The restaurant owner said to the _____ manager, "We must give the waitresses some more _____. Have Roy hire two people to _____ in clearing the tables."

responsibility
responsible
responsibly

5. Tony was such a _____ young man that his parents trusted him with the _____ of driving the family car to school because they knew he would drive _____.

convenience
convenient
inconvenient

6. It was _____ for Aliyah to return to the grocery store so she called her husband at work and asked him to go to the _____ store and pick up some butter at his earliest _____.

<table>
<tr><td>multiple
multiples
multiplied</td><td>7. There were _____ reasons why the parents of the _____ went broke, but the biggest reason is that the cost of everything they bought for the babies had to be _____ by four.</td></tr>
<tr><td>persisted
persistent
persistence</td><td>8. "If you'll let me continue," _____ the manager, who was trying to explain the rules to the new employees. You must be _____ in carrying out your duties here, and your _____ will be rewarded sooner than you can imagine."</td></tr>
<tr><td>nutrients
nutrition
nutritious</td><td>9. The most _____ energy bar I could find contained enough of all the important _____ to make sure that I was getting proper _____ even if I didn't have time to eat a whole meal.</td></tr>
<tr><td>appear
appearance
disappeared
disappearance</td><td>10. Despite the _____ of the situation, the detective decided the strange _____ of the necklace was not the result of a robbery. He was sure it had _____ while Mrs. Martin's two-year-old grandson was visiting and would soon _____ again.</td></tr>
</table>

3 Capitalization Review. Some of the words in the phrases below need to be capitalized. Rewrite each phrase correctly. Study the example before you begin. Not counting the example, you should capitalize 20 words.

1. the merry month of may   *the merry month of May* _____

2. a roll of cherry life savers   _____

3. 620 riverside drive   _____

4. her french book   _____

5. the u.s. justice department   _____

6. a can of coke   _____

7. the university of iowa   _____

8. the roaring twenties   _____

9. a dodge truck   _____

10. halloween pranks   _____

11. the canadian flag   _____

12. the oklahoma state fair   _____

4 More Work with the Ending -*ment*. To complete these sentences correctly, choose the best word from the list and add -*ment* to it.

conceal	detach	govern	misplace	punish	retire
consign	employ	involve	mistreat	require	wonder

1. Years ago, a common form of _____ for children who said naughty words was to wash their mouths out with soap.

2. Virginia searched the want ads carefully for _____ opportunities because she wanted a job that offered higher wages.

3. Many physicians suggest that one _____ for good health is drinking eight glasses of water each day.

4. Bob's _____ with the group of students who had started the fight in the gym led to his being expelled from school for three days.

5. Mr. Stuart was looking forward to _____ after twenty-five years of working hard in a machine shop, so he would have time to devote to his hobbies.

6. An expression of complete _____ appeared on Phil's face when the nurse informed him that his wife had just given birth to twin girls.

7. The manager's _____ of the brand-new computer led to its breakdown, and a repairman had to be called.

8. The Johnsons blamed the _____ for all their problems with money—even though they did not vote.

9. _____ is a necessary trait for an umpire if he is to call the action in a baseball game fairly.

10. George's _____ of important papers got him into trouble at work.

11. When Butch's _____ of stolen goods was discovered, he realized he would soon be arrested.

12. Mrs. James lost so much weight that she was able to buy all new outfits and take all of her old clothes to the _____ shop.

5 Compound Words. A compound word is made up of two or more smaller words. Fill in the blank with the letter of the correct compound word.

1. A food storage system will seal a portion of food in an _____ plastic bag.
   a. airtight   **b.** airline   **c.** airplane   **d.** airbag

2. _____ milk and yogurt are healthy sources of calcium.
   a. Fattening   **b.** Freehand   **c.** Freeform   **d.** Fat-free

3. Some of the healthier choices at the _____ include salads with low-fat dressing, grilled chicken sandwiches, and yogurt.
   a. screwdriver   **b.** driveway   **c.** drive-in   **d.** drive-through

4. Grandma Janey's doctor called in a new prescription for her at the _____.
   a. storeroom   **b.** superstore   **c.** drugstore   **d.** bookstore

5. I was sure that I had lost my cell phone _____, but I searched the whole house anyway.
   a. somewhere   **b.** someday   **c.** something   **d.** sometimes

6. Everyone in my family is _____ —even the dog—so we are all trying to get more exercise.
   a. overpaid   **b.** overweight   **c.** overtime   **d.** overcome

7. In years past, the _____ would go door-to-door and deliver bottles of milk that people ordered.
   a. workman   **b.** chairman   **c.** mailman   **d.** milkman

8. Min-hee's favorite _____ is a gray suit with a red polka-dot blouse and matching shoes.
   a. outburst   **b.** outcry   **c.** outlaw   **d.** outfit

9. On Saturday nights, we pack a picnic basket full of sandwiches and chips, and then our whole family goes to the _____ to see a double feature.
   a. drive-through   **b.** drive-in   **c.** driveway   **d** driving

10. My grandmother wears bright red lipstick, and she draws on her _____ using a soft brown pencil.
    a. eyebrows   **b.** eyesights   **c.** eyelids   **d.** eyestrains

11. Kenny lowered his electric bill by replacing every _____ in the house with an energy-efficient CFL light.
    a. candlelight   **b.** headlight   **c.** flashlight   **d.** lightbulb

12. Jerome is watching his cholesterol, so for lunch he likes to have a big salad with vegetables, tuna, nuts, and _____ Italian dressing.
    a. low-fat   **b.** lowdown   **c.** low-energy   **d.** lowlife

1 Word Review. Use the words listed below to fill in the blanks correctly. Don't forget to capitalize when necessary.

Alaska	clearance	metabolism
Alzheimer's disease	convenience store	Pilgrims
Andrew Jackson	debt	Salt Lake City
Capitol	fertility treatment	statue
census	identical twins	Thomas A. Edison

_____ **1.** chemical processes in the body that burn calories and create energy

_____ **2.** English colonists who settled in Plymouth in 1620

_____ **3.** a form that is carved or cast in stone, clay, wood, etc.

_____ **4.** a chronic disease that affects the brain and memory and gets worse over time

_____ **5.** two babies that are born from the same egg that are the same sex and share the same genes

_____ **6.** something that is owed, usually money

_____ **7.** a small market that stays open long hours

_____ **8.** a complete count of the population of a place

_____ **9.** the building in Washington, D.C., where Congress meets

_____ **10.** the capital of Utah

_____ **11.** the inventor who presented the first motion picture to the American public

_____ **12.** largest state in the U.S.; it became the 49th state in 1959

_____ **13.** medicines and medical processes used to help women have babies

_____ **14.** a sale to clear out stock

_____ **15.** the seventh president of the United States

2 Synonyms and Antonyms. State whether the following word pairs are synonyms or antonyms. Study the example before you begin.

__synonyms__	**1.** assistance—aid
_____	**2.** construction—destruction
_____	**3.** disappear—vanish
_____	**4.** previously—afterward
_____	**5.** theatrical—dramatic
_____	**6.** fluid—liquid
_____	**7.** merry—depressed
_____	**8.** noisiness—loudness
_____	**9.** polite—rude
_____	**10.** irritate—annoy
_____	**11.** persist—give up
_____	**12.** finances—money
_____	**13.** separate—detach
_____	**14.** created—ruined
_____	**15.** unwanted—popular

3 Where Might You Find These? Match the words below with the objects or places in which you would most likely find them.

Capitol building	drive-through	Massachusetts	Pennsylvania	theaters
Census Bureau	Europe	Mississippi	pharmacy	West Africa
dairy aisle	handbag	New York City	state capitals	whole grains

_____	**1.** actors and actresses	_____	**9.** Jackson
_____	**2.** Cape Cod	_____	**10.** lipstick
_____	**3.** Congress	_____	**11.** Nigeria
_____	**4.** dietary fiber	_____	**12.** population statistics
_____	**5.** fast food	_____	**13.** prescription drugs
_____	**6.** Gosselin sextuplets	_____	**14.** Statue of Liberty
_____	**7.** governors	_____	**15.** yogurt and cheese
_____	**8.** Italy		

4 Suffixes. The *-ment* and *-ness* endings you have been studying are two examples of suffixes. A *suffix* is a group of letters added to the end of a word which changes its meaning. Choose the word which best completes each sentence, and write it in the blank. As you fill in the blanks, note the six different suffixes you use.

1. "Don't ask me what looks good!" exclaimed Amrita. "You are supposed to know how to make a room look beautiful. You're the _____!"
   a. elevator **b.** decorator **c.** separator **d.** operator

2. The _____ was so shocked when his lab assistant told him that the research notes had been stolen that he refused to speak to anybody for a month.
   a. geneticist **b.** specialist **c.** racist **d.** scientist

3. The _____ of the ham caused the customer to complain, "You know, you really should warn customers that the sodium level in that ham could be harmful to their health!"
   a. greasiness **b.** spiciness **c.** saltiness **d.** tastelessness

4. "This freezer has outlived its _____," remarked Susan upon discovering that the chocolate ice cream had melted all over everything.
   a. costliness **b.** usefulness **c.** uselessness **d.** wastefulness

5. Ms. Prince told all of her employees that they needed to increase their _____ in order to lower the office overhead; otherwise, she would have to lay off several people.
   a. efficiency **b.** emergency **c.** urgency **d.** agency

6. "You don't _____ expect me to believe you're two hours late for our date because you had a flat tire?" George snapped at his guilty-looking girlfriend.
   a. desperately **b.** persistently **c.** seriously **d.** usually

7. The basketball player made up in _____ for what he lacked in physical build, and he finally won a starting spot on the team.
   a. difference **b.** insistence **c.** occurrence **d.** persistence

8. When the governor made a special guest _____ at the dinner to raise funds for cancer research, the guests applauded him for his concern.
   a. appearance **b.** assistance **c.** disappearance **d.** performance

9. The nutritionist told Mr. and Mrs. Tran that one way to help their family lose weight and get healthier is to serve smaller _____ at every meal.
   a. populations **b.** portions **c.** traditions **d.** conditions

10. "Did you find this exercise _____?" inquired the English teacher, "or did you breeze right through it?"
    a. challenging **b.** clearing **c.** considering **d.** complaining

5 Review of Capitalization Rules. Write two examples that show your understanding of each of the following rules. Study the examples before you begin.

1. Capitalize parts of the world.

    <u>South Pole</u> and <u>the Far East</u>

2. Capitalize bodies of water.

    _____ and _____

3. Capitalize people's names.

    _____ and _____

4. Capitalize the days of the week.

    _____ and _____

5. Capitalize the months of the year.

    _____ and _____

6. Capitalize holidays and holy days.

    _____ and _____

7. Capitalize the names of organizations.

    _____ and _____

8. Capitalize the names of nationalities and languages.

    _____ and _____

9. Capitalize special events and periods in history.

    _____ and _____

10. Capitalize the names of business firms and brand names of business products.

    _____ and _____

6 Compound Words.

A. Use two words from the box to form a compound word for each of the twelve descriptions. Use each word in the box only once, and cross it out when you have used it. The number of blanks for each word tells how many letters are in the compound word. Study the example before you begin.

B. When you have finished, the first letter of each compound word, reading down, should spell the name of a U.S. capital city and the state in which it is located.

ball	board	clothes	holder	left	odd	over	spring
black	bringing	hiker	ink	man	off	power	under
blot	checker	hitch	jack	man	office	sand	up

C H E C K E R B O A R D   **1.** a game board with sixty-four squares on which chess is played

___ ___ ___ ___ ___ ___ ___ ___ ___ ___ ___   **2.** a person who holds public office

___ ___ ___ ___ ___ ___ ___ ___   **3.** an unused portion of something, usually food

___ ___ ___ ___ ___ ___ ___ ___ ___ ___ ___   **4.** clothes worn next to the skin, beneath one's outer clothing

___ ___ ___ ___ ___ ___ ___ ___ ___   **5.** the workers needed to complete a task

___ ___ ___ ___ ___ ___ ___ ___ ___   **6.** a card game also called 21

___ ___ ___ ___ ___ ___ ___ ___ ___ ___   **7.** the rearing and training received during childhood

___ ___ ___ ___ ___ ___ ___ ___ ___   **8.** a character in fairy tales who puts children to sleep by sprinkling sand in their eyes

___ ___ ___ ___ ___ ___ ___ ___ ___   **9.** a person who behaves or thinks in a way that most other people consider strange

___ ___ ___ ___ ___ ___ ___ ___ ___ ___ ___   **10.** one who travels by getting free rides along the road

___ ___ ___ ___ ___ ___ ___ ___   **11.** a blotted pattern of spilled ink

___ ___ ___ ___ ___ ___ ___ ___ ___   **12.** the children in a family

City: C ___ ___ ___ ___ ___ ___ ___

State: ___ ___ ___ ___

UNIT 2
Work

Although family times may be the highlights of our week, it is in the world of work that men and women spend much of their time each day. In this unit, the subject of work is explored.

It is a sad fact, but recent studies have shown that many Americans do not like their jobs. During the Great Depression of the 1930s, however, thousands of American workers were faced with a situation that was much worse than not liking their jobs. They lost their jobs and were not able to find other work. In the reading in Lesson 6, "Voices from the Great Depression," you will learn how some people responded to this very difficult time in American history.

The Lesson 7 reading, "When John Quincy Adams Lost His Job," describes how one man reacted when he lost his job. It wasn't just any old job that he lost, for John Quincy Adams was the sixth president of the United States.

The readings for both lessons 8 and 9 are about how to get a job. Lesson 8, "Looking for a Job," offers some helpful hints about finding work. In Lesson 9, "The Job Interview," the author gives advice about how to prepare for that meeting which many people dread—the job interview.

The selection in Lesson 10 is taken from *The Adventures of Tom Sawyer*. In this reading, Mark Twain shows us how Tom Sawyer handled the situation when he had a job to do but didn't feel like working.

Words for Study

atop	assembly	caseworker	salary
we'd	foreman	psychiatrist	terrified
bonus	enrolled	suicide	references
possessions	Director	razor	application
deposit	Authority	ashamed	interview

LESSON 6
Voices from the Great Depression

by Studs Terkel

The Great Depression of the 1930s was a period of great crisis in American history. By 1932, the unemployed numbered upward of thirteen million. At least a million, perhaps as many as two million, wandered around the country in a fruitless search for work.

Here are the stories of just a few of the people who lived through these hard times.

Louis Banks, a man forced to be a hobo: 1929 was pretty bad. I hoboed, I bummed, I begged for a nickel to get somethin' to eat. When I was hoboing, I would lay on the side of the tracks and wait until I could see the train comin'. I would always carry a bottle of water and a piece of bread in my pocket, so I wouldn't starve on the way. I would ride all day and all night long in the hot sun. I'd ride atop a boxcar.

Everybody was poor. We used to take a big pot and cook food, cabbage, meat and beans together. We all set together, we made a tent. Twenty-five or thirty would be out on the side of the rail. They didn't have no mothers or sisters, they didn't have no home, they were dirty, they didn't have no food, they didn't have anything.

Peggy Terry, a woman whose family had moved from Kentucky to Oklahoma City to look for work: I first noticed the difference when we'd come home from school in the evening. My mother would send us to the soup line. We were never allowed to cuss. If you happened to be one of the first ones in line, you didn't get anything but the water that was on top. We'd ask the guy dishing out the soup to please dip down to get some meat and potatoes from the bottom of the kettle. But he wouldn't do it. So we learned to cuss. We'd say: "Dip down, goddammit."

My dad finally got a bonus and bought a used car for us to come back to Kentucky in. He said to us kids: "All of you get in the car. I want to take you and show you something." On the way, he talked about how life had been tough for us, and he said: "If you think it's been rough for us, I want you to see people that really had it rough." He took us to a place that was not to be believed.

Here were all these people living in old, rusted-out car bodies. I mean that was their home. There were people living in shacks made of orange crates. One family with a whole lot of kids were living in a piano box. This wasn't just a little section; this was maybe ten miles wide and ten miles long. People living in whatever they could junk together.

Hiram Sherman, an actor: It was rock-bottom living in New York then. It really was. You didn't count your possessions in terms of money in the bank. You counted on the fact that you had a row of empty milk bottles because these were cash. They could be turned in for a nickel deposit and that would get you on the subway. If you took any stock in yourself, you looked to see how many milk bottles you had. Two bottles: one could get you uptown, one could get you back.

Justin McCarthy, a worker in a Ford assembly plant: I sandpapered all the right-hand fenders at the Ford plant. I was paid five dollars a day. When I went to work in January, we were turning out 232 cars a day. When I was fired, four months later, we were turning out 535. Without any extra help and no increase in pay. If you wanted to go to the toilet, you had to get permission from the foreman. If he couldn't get somebody to take your place, you held it.

I made the mistake of telling the foreman I had enrolled in night courses at a local college. He said,

"Mr. Ford isn't paying people to go to college. You're fired."

Mick Shufro, Assistant Director of the Chicago Housing Authority: I remember a mother of nine children was receiving two quarts of milk. Because of a budget crisis, she was cut down to one quart. She raised hell at the relief station. The caseworker wrote her up as crazy and sent her to a psychiatrist. The psychiatrist responded as few did at the time. He said, "When this woman stops reacting the way she does, let me know. Then she would be truly insane."

Ben Isaacs, a door-to-door salesman: We tried to struggle along living day by day. Then I couldn't pay the rent. I had a little car, but I couldn't pay no license for it. I sold it for fifteen dollars in order to buy some food for the family. I didn't even have money to buy a pack of cigarettes, and I was a smoker. I didn't have a nickel in my pocket.

Finally people started to talk me into going into the relief. I didn't want to go on relief. Believe me, when I was forced to go to the office of the relief, the tears were running out of my eyes. I couldn't bear myself to take money from anybody for nothing. If it wasn't for my kids—I tell you the truth—many a time it came to my mind to go commit suicide. But somebody has to take care of those kids.

Wherever I went to get a job, I couldn't get no job, I went around selling razor blades and shoelaces. There was a day I would go over all the streets and come home with fifty cents, making a sale. That kept going until 1940. 1939 the war started. Things started to get a little better. My wife found a job in a restaurant for twenty dollars a week. Right away, I sent a letter to the relief people: I don't think I would need their help anymore. I was disgusted with relief, so ashamed. I couldn't face it anymore.

General Robert E. Wood, President of Sears, Roebuck: 1931 was worst of all. We cut, including myself. I started with a salary cut. We had to cut or we'd have gone out of business. We had to lay off thousands of people. It was terrible. I used to go through the halls of the building and these little girls—they were all terrified. I remember one Italian girl I called in.

She had a family of ten—father, mother, and eight children. She was the only one working. It was terrible. But we had to lay 'em off. I could see how frightened to death they were.

1 About the Reading. Put the letter of the best answer in the blank.

1. The introduction states that many people "wandered around the country in a fruitless search for work." *Fruitless* means _____.
   a. desperate
   b. showing no results
   c. seeking employment on farms
   d. praying for the right job offer

2. Louis Banks probably became a hobo because he _____.
   a. enjoyed traveling
   b. could not find a steady job
   c. preferred not to be tied down
   d. did not like to eat alone

3. From the selection about Peggy Terry, the reader can conclude that Peggy _____.
   a. was an only child
   b. enjoyed living in Oklahoma City
   c. lived in a house or apartment
   d. never went hungry

4. According to Hiram Sherman, it cost _____ to ride the subway in New York during the Great Depression.
   a. a nickel   **b.** a dime   **c.** a quarter   **d.** fifty cents

5. From the selection about Justin McCarthy, the reader can conclude that Justin _____.
   a. had not graduated from high school
   b. was friends with the foreman
   c. was married
   d. had to work harder the longer he worked at the Ford plant

6. Mick Shufro thinks that the psychiatrist he tells about _____.
   a. did not understand the woman's problem
   b. should have felt ashamed of himself
   c. was a better psychiatrist than most he knew
   d. should have been fired

7. According to Ben Isaacs, the hard times eased up somewhat when _____.
   a. World War II started
   b. jobs were less scarce
   c. people sold their possessions
   d. food prices went down

8. According to General Robert E. Wood, the main reaction of the people whom he had to lay off was _____.
   a. resentment   **b.** impatience   **c.** nastiness   **d.** fear

2 What Do You Think? If you had been alive during the Great Depression, what do you think your life would have been like? Be sure to include details in your description.

_____

_____

_____

_____

_____

_____

_____

_____

_____

3 Synonyms. On the blank to the right, write the synonym for the first word in the line. Study the example before you begin.

1. **possess:**	borrow	deserve	desire	own	**own**
2. **doubtful:**	uncertain	uncommon	unfair	unwilling	
3. **ashamed:**	sensitive	outclassed	disgraced	terrified	
4. **permit:**	allow	consider	deposit	enroll	
5. **recently:**	generally	hourly	lately	seldom	
6. **terrify:**	disturb	frighten	injure	reject	
7. **easygoing:**	careless	normal	outgoing	relaxed	
8. **alter:**	assist	change	repair	undo	
9. **gloomy:**	cold-eyed	dejected	hearty	serious	
10. **scatter:**	disable	discharge	disperse	dispose	
11. **moral:**	story	ending	fable	lesson	
12. **concept:**	idea	law	rule	suggestion	

4 The Suffix -ful. To complete these sentences, choose the correct word from the list and add -ful to it. Study the example before you begin.

event	fear	force	plate	play	regret	✓scoop

1. Mrs. Lopez asked the clerk to measure out a _____**scoopful**_____ of blueberry jelly beans, which she planned to share with her son.

2. Jackie's _____ new puppy nipped at her heels as they ran through the park.

3. Winning the contest certainly made Dennis's day very _____, but he was so _____ of becoming seasick that he turned down the all-expenses-paid cruise to Hawaii.

4. "You have excellent references," explained Ms. Thor as she skimmed Philip's application, "but I'm afraid you just aren't _____ enough to be a foreman; our workers would take advantage of you in a minute."

5. "Why should I feel _____?" snapped the waitress to her manager. "If the customer had behaved politely, I would never have dumped the _____ of French fries in his lap."

5 The Suffix -less. To complete these sentences, choose the correct word from the list and add -less to it. Study the example before you begin.

age	blame	fear	heart	meaning	mind	✓shame

1. The _____**shameless**_____ traitor just shrugged his shoulders when, during an interview, a reporter called him a disgrace to his country.

2. "How can you be so _____!" exclaimed Jane when her former boss refused to give her a good reference because he couldn't bear the thought of her working for anyone else.

3. Ninety-one-year-old Mr. Benjamin had so much energy that his neighbors regarded him as one of those _____ human beings who would outlive them all.

4. "This discussion is _____," Anne said to her business partners, "if you refuse to see that we aren't entirely _____ for the terrible working conditions around here."

5. When Hiram dashed into the burning animal shelter to rescue the trapped kittens, some bystanders praised him as a _____ hero. Others, however, called him _____ because the odds of his getting out of the building alive were very slim.

6 Review of Capitalization Rules. Capitalize the words in the following sentences correctly. The number at the end of each sentence tells you how many words to capitalize. If necessary, review the rules you've studied so far in Lessons 3 and 4.

More about the Great Depression

1. october 29, 1929, is known as black tuesday in american history books; that was the day the stock market on wall street in new york city hit bottom. (9)

2. during the first and worst years of the depression, the people turned to washington for help; and when the president of the united states did not offer the necessary assistance, they voted him out of office. (5)

3. in 1931, a man who worked for the public school system in chicago begged the governor of illinois to help feed the city's children during the summer. (3)

4. in the 1930s, our main meal was something uncle robert called *shipwreck:* heated campbell's tomato soup poured over ritz crackers. (5)

5. not only was there no money during the great depression, there was no rain. in georgia, a black man was paid ten dollars to pray for rain. in new york, an indian tribe revived their rain-prayer dance for the first time in forty years. (10)

6. a texas farmer, angry because his crops were drying up from lack of rain, jumped on his tractor and began to drive in circles around his fields. as he drove, he spluttered, "i know this won't do any good, but i've got to do something." (5)

7. on december 7, 1941, americans were shocked to learn that the japanese had bombed pearl harbor in hawaii. shortly afterward, congress declared war on japan. (10)

8. the great depression came to an end when congress voted huge sums of money for producing goods that the united states would need to fight in world war II. (8)

Words for Study

Quincy	undertook	slavery	union
election	trickled	abuse	James Polk
desirable	Congressman	symbol	coma
bitterly	fierce	pimples	tomb
series	furies	promise	classified
instance	ex-president	Alabama	abbreviation

When John Quincy Adams Lost His Job

by Lawrence Lader

In 1828, John Quincy Adams lost his job. He had been president of the United States for four years, and now he had been defeated in the 1828 election by Andrew Jackson. Losing the election greatly depressed John Quincy Adams who could not adjust to this painful defeat. He shut himself off from the world in his Quincy, Massachusetts, home and wrote, "I have no real reason for wishing to live when every thought I have about the future makes death desirable." Bitterly, Adams complained, "My whole life has been a series of disappointments. I can scarcely remember a single instance of success in anything that I ever undertook."

Short, overweight, and almost completely bald, John Quincy Adams was old before his time. He had many ailments. His hand shook almost beyond control when he wrote. He complained about his bloodshot eyes which were so weak and swollen that tears often trickled from the corners. His voice, which was always shrill, tended to crack whenever he spoke. He slept little and badly, and his diary was filled with complaints of "disturbed sleep—full of tossings."

Another problem was Adams's temper, which was extremely short. One Congressman described it as "fierce as ten furies, terrible as hell." Adams himself

admitted in his diary that he was forever having to work hard to control his temper.

Then, in 1830, a group of devoted friends convinced Adams to run for Congress. Adams felt as if he had been born a new man. He was sixty-three years old, a retired president, and the son of the second president of the United States. Never before and never since has a former president of the United States run for Congress.

Adams won his election and entered Congress. There he would serve for the next eighteen years—until the end of his life. Instead of the peace and quiet sought by George Washington and other ex-presidents, John Quincy Adams would carve out a brand-new career for himself. Though he had carefully avoided the slavery issue during his White House years, Adams now plunged into it with all his heart, drawing much anger and debate around his head. No other former president would experience such abuse. Newspapers even branded him the "Mad Man from Massachusetts."

John Quincy Adams became a one-man symbol of the struggle against slavery. Day after day, with surprising energy, he held the floor of Congress, his shrill voice slashing away at his enemies. Even though he suffered from a bad cough, pimples, and boils, he would arise early each morning to prepare his work for the day.

Adams's hard work to end slavery brought an increasing flood of angry and threatening letters to his desk. "Your damned guts will be cut out in the dark" warned a writer from Georgia. "On the first day of May, I promise to cut your throat from ear to ear," threatened an Alabama writer.

In spite of these dark threats, Adams worked on in his efforts to end slavery which he had once described as "the great and foul stain upon the North American Union." Slowly but surely, his efforts began to win the praise of others who were also devoted to ending slavery in the United States.

In 1842, the South suffered its first important defeat in Congress—a defeat that had been brought about mainly through the work of John Quincy Adams.

In a letter to his wife, Adams's assistant described this Southern defeat: "This is the first victory over the slaveholders in a body ever yet gained since the founding of the government and from this time their downfall takes its date."

On Monday, February 21, 1848, Adams, now eighty-one, reached Congress early as usual. James Polk, who was now president of the United States, had just received the treaty of peace with Mexico. A roll call was going on, and the House was filled with clatter. Suddenly, a member seated near Adams saw the old man's face redden, while his right hand clutched at the corner of his desk. Then he slumped over.

Someone cried out and caught Adams in his arms. They carried him to the cleared area in front of the Speaker's table, where he was placed on a couch and moved to the Speaker's room. For a few minutes Adams revived. Leaning close, a fellow Congressman heard Adams say, "This is the end of earth, but I am at peace."

Meanwhile, Adams's wife arrived, but Adams had fallen into a coma and gave no sign of recognizing her. He remained in a coma through Washington's birthday and at 7:20 on the evening of February 23 passed away.

The service three days later was a great public event. Thousands of people filed by his coffin while he lay in state in the House. Southern leaders joined the North in paying honor to Adams. Then the body was taken to Boston, where thousands more paid their last respects.

Adams was buried in Quincy, Massachusetts—in the old family tomb in the churchyard. At the last moment a southern congressman in the funeral party stepped forward and, stooping before the Adams vault, called out, "Good-bye, Old Man!"

1 About the Reading. Put the letter of the best answer in the blank.

1. The title of this reading selection refers to the job that John Quincy Adams lost. What job did he lose?
   a. mayor of Quincy
   b. congressman from Georgia
   c. governor of Massachusetts
   d. president of the United States

2. When Adams lost this job, he felt _____.
   a. dejected   **b.** fierce   **c.** puzzled   **d.** relieved

3. Then, receiving encouragement from his _____, he decided to run for Congress.
   a. friends   **b.** father   **c.** wife   **d.** children

4. While in Congress, Adams was called the "Mad Man from Massachusetts" because he _____.
   a. did not retire to peace and quiet as other ex-presidents had
   b. did not take very good care of himself
   c. fought to end slavery
   d. had a terrible temper

5. Just before he died, Adams said he was "at peace." He probably felt this way because he had _____.
   a. succeeded in becoming famous
   b. finished all he had set out to do
   c. helped to end the war with Mexico
   d. made important strides toward ending slavery

6. Adams was buried in _____.
   a. Washington, D.C.   **b.** Massachusetts   **c.** Vermont   **d.** New York

7. The southern Congressman who called out "Good-bye, Old Man" probably _____.
   a. did not know Adams's name
   b. thought Adams was too old to serve in Congress
   c. thought Adams was silly not to retire after being defeated by Jackson
   d. admired Adams

8. The author of this reading selection seems to _____ John Quincy Adams.
   a. disagree with
   b. admire
   c. have been a personal friend of
   d. lack respect for

An arithmetic problem. In what year did Adams become president of the United States? _____

2 Symbols. A *symbol* is a sign that stands for an object or an idea. All words are symbols. One well-known symbol is the national flag. To most people, the flag of their nation means "my country." Below are two sets of commonly used symbols. Match the symbols with what they stand for.

CO_2	H	scales	Uncle Sam	ⓘ
four-leaf clover	red and white striped pole	skull and crossbones	white cross	♫

_____ **1.** barber shop   _____ **6.** information

_____ **2.** carbon dioxide   _____ **7.** justice

_____ **3.** first aid   _____ **8.** music

_____ **4.** good luck   _____ **9.** poison

_____ **5.** hospital   _____ **10.** United States

Sometimes animals are used as symbols. Match these animals with what they stand for.

bat	bee or ant	eel	lamb	owl
beaver	dove	fox	mule	ox or bull

_____ **1.** blindness   _____ **6.** slipperiness

_____ **2.** busyness   _____ **7.** slyness

_____ **3.** eagerness   _____ **8.** strength

_____ **4.** gentleness   _____ **9.** stubbornness

_____ **5.** peace   _____ **10.** wisdom

3 Word Families. Use the words in each set listed at the left to complete these sentences.

elected election

1. After the _____, the governor felt so exhausted that he almost wished the voters hadn't _____ him to serve a second term.

adjust adjustments

2. "I've had to make a lot of _____ in my time," wept Grandfather to his grandson, "but I don't think I'll ever _____ to living without your grandmother."

refer reference

3. "In _____ to your question about John Quincy Adams," responded the teacher to her students, "let's _____ to our history book."

prefer
preference

4. When the waiter asked Peggy if she would _____ French or Italian dressing on her tossed salad, she replied, "I don't really have a _____."

slippery
slipperiness

5. The weather forecaster, who was predicting freezing rain, told his listeners, "Those of you who walk to work, watch out for the _____ sidewalks. And those of you who drive, watch out for the _____ of the roads."

hearty
heartily
heartless

6. "After such a _____ meal at the Marshes' housewarming party," laughed Rocco _____, "I think it would be _____ of us not to invite them to our Saturday picnic."

stubborn
stubbornly
stubbornness

7. "I am not _____!" Isaac insisted _____ after his daughter had stated that the family's crisis was caused by his _____.

applied
applicant
application

8. While filling out the _____ for the chef's position at Lowland Hotel, the _____ asked the desk clerk if many people had _____.

coward
cowardly
cowardliness

9. "Not only has your _____ in the line of duty cost many brave men their lives today," said the commander coldly, "but the _____ excuses you make to explain your actions make me realize that you're a _____ through and through."

usual
usually
unusual
unusually

10. "You just don't seem like your _____ self these days, Justin," commented his sister, who _____ didn't mind _____ long periods of quiet but was becoming increasingly worried because Justin's silence seemed so _____.

4 Looking for a Job. Most ex-presidents don't have to read the classified ads if they want to continue working. Most of us do. Study the following ads taken from the classified section of a daily newspaper and then answer the questions.

ANSWERING SERVICE OPERATOR – Good telephone manner a must, 7:30a.m.– 1p.m. Mon. thru Fri. Call 555–2226.	BUS PERSON PART TIME WEEKENDS No experience necessary. Must be 16 or older, for appl. call Rolling Hills Country Club 555-8381 (Closed Mondays)	DRIVERS, If you are seriously thinking of making driving your career. Apply in person: Carson's Yellow Cab, 155 Main St.	Manager needed for better ladies sportswear shop. Experience necessary. Phone 555-1977 for an appointment.
ASSISTANT SWIM COACH 5 days a week, hours 5–7p.m. meets are held on Saturdays. Season Sept–March. For details call YMCA 555-1000	CONSTRUCTION "Jack-of-all-Trades" Must have exper. in light carpentry & have ability to make adjustments & small repairs on call-backs. Phone 555-5100 days, 9–6.	GAS STATION Full Time Manager New Milford area Call Ph: 555-0650	RESTAURANT – Sandwich & Salad bar person. 3 evenings per week, 3–10p.m. Apply in person, Plain Jane's Restaurant.
ASSISTANT COOKS — 4 shifts-week, will train. Ideal for students Apply in person: Pickles Restaurant.	COOK wanted for Day Care Center, 10a.m.–1p.m. Mon–Fri. Call for interview: 555–2480	GRILL PERSONS- Full & part time. Good wages & vacations. Apply in person Combs Restaurant, 113 Mill Plain Rd.	SWIMMING POOL – Local pool company looking for young and strong person to help with pool construction. Call 555-0777 bet. 10am-5pm
BARTENDER, part time. days or nights. Apply in person: Cheers, 5 Elm St.	COUNTER HELP WANTED for auto parts store Apply in person between 1–4p.m. 139 Main St.	GROUNDS WORKER Needed for tree company. Will train if necessary. Good wages, call 555-8790.	WAITER-WAITRESS wanted for morning shift or supper hour shifts. Please apply in person. Windmill Diner: 14 Mall Plain Rd

1. Because space is so tight, many abbreviations are used in classified ads. What do the following abbreviations stand for? Study the example before you begin.

   a. Mon. _____Monday_____   **d.** appt. _____

   b. Fri. _____   **e.** bet. _____

   c. Sept. _____   **f.** & _____

2. Which ad states an age requirement? _____

3. Which two ads state that experience is necessary? _____

4. Why do you think some of these ads state that the applicant must apply in person?

_____

_____

5. If you had to work and these ads were the only employment opportunities open to you, which of these jobs would you apply for? Be sure to include reasons in your answer.

_____

_____

_____

_____

5 Can You Crack the Code? Each group of letters spells the name of an American president, but the names have been concealed by a code in which a new set of letters has been used in place of the normal letters. The code is the same for all the words. When you have guessed the name of the president, use these letters to help you figure out the names of the remaining presidents. The first item has been done for you.

1. **J A M E S   P O L K**
   B X C K G   W Z P S

2. _____   _____
   Y K Z O Y K   E X G U F T Y M Z T

3. _____   _____
   B Z U T   Q   S K T T K J L

4. _____   _____   _____
   B Z U T   V H F T R L   X J X C G

5. _____   _____
   X T J O K E   B X R S G Z T

6. _____   _____
   X D O X U X C   P F T R Z P T

7. _____   _____
   B Z U T   X J X C G

8. _____   _____
   M U Z C X G   B K Q Q K O G Z T

9. _____   _____
   B X C K G   C X J F G Z T

10. _____   _____
    B X C K G   C Z T O Z K

Words for Study

technology	effective	blogs	nouns
overwhelming	recommendations	professional	flexible
embrace	attachments	alumni	freelance
communicate	requirements	strategies	assignments
potential	networking	resumé	benefits
available	social	verbs	telecommuting

L E S S O N   8
Looking for a Job?

The job search of the 21st century is much different from the job hunt of the 20th century. Technology continues to improve by leaps and bounds. Many job searches are now performed online.

An endless supply of online resources offers advice, help, and tips for the job seeker. The sheer amount of information can be overwhelming. Job seekers who are less at ease with technology can end up feeling lost. However, the facts can't be denied. The Internet is increasingly important to today's job search, and technology is likely to play a major role for years to come.

Instead of thinking of technology as an enemy, embrace it as a friend. The Internet puts a wealth of free resources at your fingertips. You can find the most up-to-date information online. You can communicate with other job seekers, with potential employers, and with experts in your field. You don't even have to leave your house to do so.

Preparing for the Job Search

You may have a tough time sorting through all the career advice available online. One effective way to wade through the sea of information is to trust the experts. Visit well-known career sites, such as http://www.jobhuntersbible.com or http://www.rileyguide.com. Explore their lists of links and recommendations. General career websites offer a wide range of useful tools. You can find personality tests, interview tips, company profiles, and salary guidelines, among other things. This information can be very helpful to today's job seekers.

Many jobs are listed online, either on job-search sites like Careerbuilder.com or Idealist.org, or on a company's own website. Most major newspapers post their classified ads online. Online ads can be very useful. Job seekers can search for certain key words or job titles without reading through every listing. That can save a lot of time.

In order to apply online, you may need to learn new skills. You may have to send attachments over e-mail, upload files to a website, or fill out electronic forms. Make sure to send your information in the

manner requested. If you need to learn how to meet the requirements, take the time to do so. Following directions shows that you are serious about meeting an employer's needs. If you don't follow the rules, most employers will notice.

Networking

Sometimes the Internet can seem impersonal. However, it is actually a major tool for building personal ties. Meeting people, creating contacts, and social "networking" have always been important parts of the job hunt. Many job openings are never offered to the public. They are filled on the basis of personal connections.

Online networking can be less overwhelming than trying to connect with strangers in person. And it can have the same results. It is common now to form bonds and relationships through e-mails, blogs, and chats.

To get started, search for professional groups, alumni sites, and other online career groups. Visit their message boards, blogs, and chat rooms. "Listen in" at first if you don't feel comfortable joining the discussion. Make note of people who may be useful to contact. Always make sure to communicate in a professional manner, no matter how informal a group may seem. Employers sometimes listen in on such discussions. An employer may contact you if you present yourself in a successful manner. But be aware that some employers search online job sites to see if their own employees are applying for jobs with other companies.

Remember that public information is easy to find these days. A simple Internet search is all it takes. Social networks such as MySpace and Facebook can be great career networking sources. But even if you don't intend to use your personal profile to attract employers, an employer could still stumble across your information. You may want to think twice before you upload silly photographs or personal

stories meant for your friends' eyes only. If you have a goofy e-mail address or user name, you may want to change it. Each bit of information you supply says something about who you are. Ask yourself, "Does it say what I want it to say about me?"

New Strategies

Some websites allow you to post your resumé online for employers to view. But remember, new opportunities often require new strategies. Some employers use special computer programs to scan online resumés. The programs search for certain key words related to a job. In the past, resumés needed to include strong action verbs. Now, they must also include the right nouns. As technology continues to change, applicants' strategies will also need to shift and adjust.

Workplace Trends

Technology has affected the workplace itself. It has changed how people do their jobs. It has also changed hiring and working patterns. A growing number of companies now embrace flexible work arrangements. Some companies hire freelance employees, who work from home or elsewhere. Freelancers perform job assignments for an agreed upon pay rate. They are self-employed and are not hired on as part of the staff. That means they do not receive benefits from the company. Freelancers often earn a higher hourly rate because of that fact. Some companies find it easier and more cost-effective to hire freelance employees. Many freelancers like having the freedom to work from home, for more than one employer, or for higher pay.

Telecommuting is another workplace trend. Employees who telecommute are part of a company's staff. They are not freelance workers. However, they work from home for at least some part of the workweek. They use technology to send information between the office and home. Telecommuting cuts down on the cost of gas and on time spent stuck in traffic. It could help combat global warming if enough people reduce their daily drives to and from work.

In 2001, about 13 million people in the U.S. worked under flexible work arrangements. They worked as freelancers, short-term workers, contract workers, or on-call workers. Most were pleased with their work arrangements.

Job seekers looking for flexible employment need to be aware of scams. Telecommuting and work-from-home scams are fairly common. If an opportunity promises lots of money for very little work, it is most likely a scam. Most scams sound too good to be true. That's because they are! Don't be fooled.

Embrace Change

It is clear that technology has changed both the traditional job search and the job market. Instead of running scared, take the opportunity to learn and benefit from such changes. Doing so isn't as hard as it seems. Plus, you will gain useful skills that you can bring to the workplace.

1 About the Reading. Six of the statements below disagree with the advice offered in the reading. Rewrite these statements to agree with the advice. Be sure that your rewritten statements include the reason given for the piece of advice. For the two statements that already agree with the author, just copy the statements on the lines provided. Study the example before you begin.

1. There is no reason to learn about technology because it is unlikely to play a major role in job searches in the future.

   You should learn about technology because it is likely to play a major role in job searches in the future.

2. When searching for career advice online, you should visit every website available to you.

   _____

   _____

3. Make sure to send your information in the manner requested. Following directions shows that you are serious about meeting an employer's needs.

   _____

   _____

4. If people in an online networking group communicate in an informal manner, you should do the same.

   _____

   _____

5. Don't worry about posting silly pictures and personal stories online; no employer will ever stumble upon your Facebook page.

_____

_____

6. Job seekers looking for flexible employment need to be aware of telecommuting and work-from-home scams, which are fairly common.

_____

_____

7. Once you learn certain job-searching strategies, you won't have to learn any new strategies.

_____

_____

8. In 2001, most people who had flexible work arrangements were not pleased with those arrangements.

_____

_____

_____

2 Antonyms. Circle the antonym for the first word in each line. Study the example before you begin.

1. flexible:	traditional	effective	general	(strict)
2. overwhelming:	manageable	great	overpowering	tired
3. comfortable:	familiar	at ease	uneasy	common
4. embrace:	hug	welcome	reject	shrug
5. professional:	casual	outgoing	proper	unaffected
6. required:	desirable	undesirable	unnecessary	unusual
7. actual:	commonplace	evil	imagined	unlikely
8. up-to-date:	timely	old	above	tradition
9. social:	personal	popular	pointless	unfriendly
10. endless:	ongoing	limited	continue	stop
11. advice:	warning	guideline	tips	counselor
12. increasingly:	major	minor	less	more

3 Who Does What? Match each person or group listed below with the correct description. If you have trouble completing the exercise, look up any difficult words in a dictionary.

✓alumni	commuter	on-call worker	short-term worker
applicant	expert	potential employer	social networker
blogger	freelancer	scammer	telecommuter

___alumni___   **1.** This group of people used to attend the same college or university.

_____   **2.** This person knows a great deal about a certain field, industry, or career and often offers advice on the subject.

_____   **3.** This person agrees to report for work on short notice if a regular employee calls in sick or if there is an emergency.

_____   **4.** This person works on certain job assignments from home or elsewhere but is not hired on as part of a company's staff.

_____   **5.** This person tries to trick job seekers by offering them a fake chance to make a lot of money for very little work.

_____   **6.** This person writes an online journal, known as a blog.

_____   **7.** This person works from home or elsewhere for at least part of the workweek but is part of a company's staff.

_____   **8.** This person tries to fill a job opening by handing in a resumé or job form.

_____   **9.** This person spends time forming personal ties, creating contacts, and getting to know other people.

_____   **10.** This person fills a job opening for a brief time period.

_____   **11.** This person drives to work.

_____   **12.** This person might offer you a job.

4 The Suffix -ly. Many people claim that it's not what you do that's important—it's how you do it. Words that end in -ly usually tell how something is done or said. In the following sentences, put the letter of the best answer in the blank.

1. Jerome couldn't believe it, but it was true: he was _____ going to get a job offer.
   a. formerly   **b.** eagerly   **c.** fairly   **d.** actually

2. During the interview, it had become _____ clear that he had all the skills that the employer wanted.
   a. doubtfully   **b.** faithfully   **c.** increasingly   **d.** likely

3. As soon as he realized that the job was his, Jerome wanted the interview to end. But it seemed to drag on _____.
   a. clearly   **b.** endlessly   **c.** gratefully   **d.** especially

4. "Jerome," the interviewer asked, "please don't take this _____, but why have you been out of work for so long?"
   a. commonly   **b.** heartlessly   **c.** thoughtfully   **d.** personally

5. Jerome knew this was a _____ dangerous question and wasn't sure how to answer.
   a. coldly   **b.** oddly   **c.** potentially   **d.** impersonally

6. "The last job I applied for didn't seem to be a good match," Jerome replied _____. "I guess they didn't take me seriously."
   a. nervously   **b.** regularly   **c.** equally   **d.** formally

7. "Why in the world would they not take you seriously?" the interviewer asked _____.
   a. bizarrely   **b.** stupidly   **c.** shyly   **d.** uneasily

8. "Well, when they asked me whether I was comfortable working _____, I told them I'd be good at it since I practice yoga," Jerome said sheepishly.
   a. emotionally   **b.** flexibly   **c.** thoroughly   **d.** efficiently

9. "Well, I guess I can see why they wouldn't take that answer seriously," the interviewer said _____. "But at our company, we like an employee with a sense of humor."
   a. grandly   **b.** laughingly   **c.** shamefully   **d.** magically

10. "Then you will _____ like me!" Jerome responded with a relieved smile.
    a. disapprovingly   **b.** professionally   **c.** especially   **d.** distractedly

5 Capitalization Rules: Part 3. Don't feel distressed. You have only four more capitalization rules to learn now. After you have studied these new rules, capitalize the words in the sentences correctly. Remember that the number after each sentence tells you how many words need to be capitalized. Don't forget to apply all the rules for capitalization that you have studied.

11. **Capitalize the first word and all important words in titles of books, plays, movies, TV shows, magazines, newspapers, stories, poems, works of art, and pieces of music.**

    Examples: books......................................The Lord of the Rings

    plays ....A Raisin in the Sun

    movies ....It's a Wonderful Life

    TV shows...............................Saturday Night Live

    magazines...............................Time, TV Guide, Better Homes and Gardens

    newspapers.............................Chicago Sun-Times

    stories....................................Hearts and Hands

    poems.....................................Stopping by Woods on a Snowy Evening

    works of art ....Last Supper, The Thinker

    pieces of music ....Bridge Over Troubled Water

12. **Capitalize names referring to the one God of a religion, religions and their followers, and major religious writings.**

    Examples: the one God of a religion.......God, Lord, Messiah, Buddha, Allah

    religions..................................Christianity, Judaism, Islam

    followers of religions ....Muslims, Mormons, Catholics, Jews

    religious writings....................Bible, Koran, Talmud, the Old Testament, the Book of Job

    Note: Do not capitalize the word *god* when it is used to refer to a religion with many gods.

    Example: The Greek god Pan watched over flocks, fields, and forests.

13. **Capitalize course names followed by a number and language courses.**

    Examples: Math 153, History 101, Italian

    Note: Do not capitalize the names of school subjects.

    Examples: history, reading, art

14. **Capitalize East, West, North, and South when they refer to recognized sections of the country or of the world.**

    Examples: the South, the Middle East

    Note: Do not capitalize these words when they tell directions.

    Examples: Many geese head south for the winter. Colorado is west of Illinois.

1. in english class on thursday, the students groaned when mr. fisher told them they would have to have completed reading *a tale of two cities* by monday. (10)

2. while traveling through the south, the trentons stopped at the stony brook motel, which was located on the east end of beech avenue in memphis. (9)

3. francis scott key wrote "the star-spangled banner" during the war of 1812 while he was a prisoner on a british warship. (9)

4. when peggy won the fishing contest sponsored by hickock county, her picture appeared in the *grand island daily times.* (8)

5. mrs. ritz wrote a letter to the department of transportation in washington, d.c., to complain about the condition of the highways in parts of new england. (9)

6. upon reading his application for smothers business college, louise asked mick, "just tell me why you plan to enroll in typing II when you nearly failed typing I last year at walnut hills high school." (13)

7. mr. east drove north five blocks along north street when he should have driven south five blocks along south street, so he completely missed his interview with the manager of west branch savings & loan. (10)

8. when jesse took a religion course in college, he studied christianity, judaism, and islam by reading selections from the bible, the talmud, and the koran. (8)

9. the american red cross and the sons of italy combined their efforts to offer relief to those who lost their homes in the flood by opening a shelter in the basement of moosewood city hall. (9)

10. leafing through the pages of *family circle* magazine, james jefferson noticed an unusual recipe for boston cream pie which he considered making for the helping hand club's autumn bake sale. (9)

6 Online Job Advertisement. Below is a sample online job advertisement. Read the advertisement and answer the questions that follow.

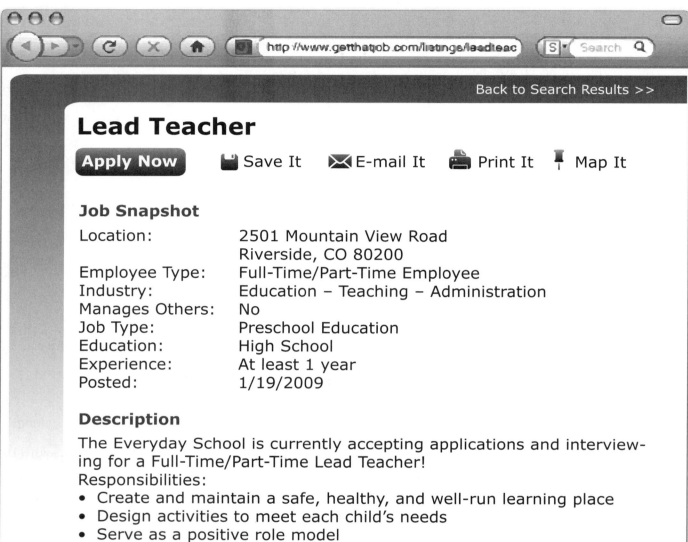

Back to Search Results >>

Lead Teacher

Apply Now   💾 Save It   ✉ E-mail It   🖨 Print It   📌 Map It

Job Snapshot

Location:	2501 Mountain View Road Riverside, CO 80200
Employee Type:	Full-Time/Part-Time Employee
Industry:	Education – Teaching – Administration
Manages Others:	No
Job Type:	Preschool Education
Education:	High School
Experience:	At least 1 year
Posted:	1/19/2009

Description

The Everyday School is currently accepting applications and interviewing for a Full-Time/Part-Time Lead Teacher!
Responsibilities:
• Create and maintain a safe, healthy, and well-run learning place
• Design activities to meet each child's needs
• Serve as a positive role model
• Build positive relationships with students' families
• Maintain a professional attitude
HOURS: 8:30 a.m.-5:30 p.m. M-F or 8:30 a.m.-12:30 p.m. M-F

Requirements

• At least 18 hours of related coursework
  (Education, Early Childhood, Child Development, Psychology, etc.)
• Prefer a degree in a related field
• Experience working with children under the age of 6 years

Compensation:

• Hourly – based on experience and education.
  Benefits for full-time teachers only.

Click Here to Find Salary Information for This Job

1. You can click on blue, underlined links on a webpage to perform certain actions. Describe the seven actions you can perform on this webpage.

   _____

   _____

   _____

   _____

   _____

   _____

2. What does this employer state about a college degree?

   _____

   _____

   _____

3. Does this job require you to manage or oversee other workers?

   _____

   _____

   _____

4. What two things are requirements for the job?

   _____

   _____

   _____

5. What three things affect the amount of salary you earn?

   _____

   _____

   _____

6. Does the job require you work with students or parents or both?

   _____

   _____

   _____

7. If you want to work as a full-time teacher, what are the job hours?

_____

_____

_____

If you want to work as a part-time teacher, what are the job hours?

_____

_____

_____

8. Would you rather work part-time or full-time? Why?

_____

_____

_____

9. If you wanted to figure out how to drive to the interview, what link on the page would help you?

_____

_____

_____

7 More Work with the Suffix -*ly*. To add -*ly* to these words, change the *y* to *i* and add -*ly*. Study the example before you begin.

1. angry   **angrily** _____

2. hearty _____

3. merry _____

4. cheery _____

5. mighty _____

6. lazy _____

7. steady _____

8. crazy _____

9. dreamy _____

10. unworthy _____

11. guilty _____

12. dizzy _____

Words for Study

ensure	circumstances	demonstrate	negotiate
scheduled	qualities	conference	eligible
articles	illegal	appealing	graduate
material	inappropriate	valuable	volunteer
open-ended	front-runners	policy	discriminate

LESSON 9
The Job Interview

Preparing yourself for a job interview is a key way to ensure success. Once you have an interview scheduled, research the company and position thoroughly. Visit the company's website and explore what it has to offer. Does the company print a newsletter? If so, read the most recent issues. Search the Internet for news articles about the company. Take notes on the material you find. Make sure that you know enough about the position and the employer to be able to prove your interest and investment in the job.

Review the job description and pay attention to the key points mentioned in the ad. Then try this exercise. Take a piece of paper and divide it in half. On one half, write down the skills and abilities the employer is seeking. On the other half, write down specific examples that match your skills to those needs. If there are skills you don't have, think of other skills you do have that make up for that lack. For example, you can point out that you are a fast learner. You can explain that you are eager to pick up new skills and will work hard to do so.

Doing Your Homework

Use the Internet to research commonly asked interview questions. This can help you avoid drawing a blank during the actual interview. Be

ready for some broad open-ended questions and some very specific questions. An interviewer might begin by asking you to tell a little about yourself. Later on, he or she might describe a specific situation and ask how you would handle yourself under those circumstances.

Interviewers often ask you to name your strengths and weaknesses and to explain how those qualities have affected your job performance in the past. It's best to prepare an answer in advance and to think of a weakness that is really a hidden strength. Some interviewers will want you to give examples to back up your answers throughout the interview. So it's good to think back on past experiences you may want to mention. Again, take notes so that you can remember and review your examples.

It is illegal for interviewers to ask certain questions. They should not ask you about on-the-job injuries and legal claims, for example. They should not ask you about your medical or mental health record. You can learn more about illegal interview questions by contacting your state's Department of Human Rights or your local employment office.

Think of a few questions that you can ask during the interview. An interviewer will almost always ask you if you have questions. It is far better to have one or two questions prepared than to have none. Try to tailor the questions to the specific job or company. Make sure not to ask inappropriate or overly personal questions. Unless the interviewer brings up salary, don't ask about money until you receive an actual job offer.

Finally, practice answering and asking questions in front of someone else or in front of a mirror. Pay attention to your body language and try to calm your nerves.

Types of Interviews

There are several different ways in which an employer can interview an applicant. Screening interviews happen early in the hiring process. They narrow down the field of applicants to a few front-runners. Employers may or may not choose to do screening interviews. If they do, they may interview applicants by phone or ask them to come into the office. Put as much effort into a screening interview as you would into a regular interview. It never hurts to impress people early on! If you get a phone interview, make sure to have your resumé and notes handy so you can refer to them easily.

Most jobs require a round of formal selection interviews. These can be one-on-one, or they can be run by a group of people. Some interviews include a few potential co-workers, who try to judge how well you would fit with the team. Some interviews

take place at a restaurant, over a meal, to get a sense of how you handle social situations. A work-sample interview usually requires you to demonstrate your skills by giving a speech, teaching a class, answering phones, or doing some other task related to the job position. Selection interviews may take place in person, by phone, by video conference, or over the Internet.

Creating a Good Impression

Make sure to dress up for your interview. Neatness and appearance do matter. Dress a little above the actual dress code for the position. Have a decent haircut, clean fingernails, and fresh breath. Make sure to arrive on time, or early. Go by yourself and bring any requested support materials. Shake hands firmly with each interviewer.

Regardless of the interview style, you always want to present yourself in a pleasant, appealing manner. Relate to the interviewers before, during, and after the interview. Sell yourself as a natural, valuable part of the team. Be direct, make eye contact with everyone, and remember to smile.

Before you leave, ask when the interviewer plans to make a hiring decision. That way, you will know when to expect a response. Ask whether you can follow up with a phone call and when would be a good time to check back. Make sure to respect the employer's wishes on this matter. You don't want to seem too pushy.

After the Interview

It is good form to send a thank-you note after an interview. Sometimes a thank-you e-mail is fitting. In your note, thank the interviewer for his or her time. Repeat, briefly, why you are excited about the job opportunity. Maybe mention a detail from the interview. Keep your thank-you note simple, polite, and to the point.

While waiting to hear back from the interviewer, it is a good idea to research the general salary range for the position. That way, you will be prepared if the employer makes an offer. One good source for this information is http://www.careeronestop.org. Some employers also list salary ranges on their Human Resources webpage.

When offering you a job, an employer may tell you there is a fixed starting rate for the position or may ask you to name your price. You can try to name a figure close to the top of the salary range, but be prepared to adjust the amount if needed. You may want to ask about the company's policy on raises as well. Sometimes it's hard to tell whether or not there is room to negotiate salary. But if an employer tells you directly that there is no negotiating, accept the statement as fact and don't try.

After the interview, you should also prepare any questions you have about any benefits that come with the position. Benefits may or may not include health care, life insurance, paid holidays and sick days, retirement plans, and other extras. Don't forget to factor benefits into your thinking when considering salary.

Remember that you do not have to accept a job offer right away. Sometimes it makes sense to take a little time and think over everything. Make sure that you don't have any other questions and that you are happy with the salary and benefits. Most employers understand that applicants may want to get back to them with an answer.

1 About the Reading. Put the letter of the correct answer in the blank.

1. Unless the interviewer brings up the subject of salary, the proper time to bring up pay and benefits is _____.
   a. after you have accepted the job
   b. at the beginning of the interview
   c. once you've received the job offer
   d. never

2. The subtitle "Doing Your Homework" refers to _____.
   a. making sure that you have included your education history in your resumé
   b. writing an essay about your strengths and weaknesses
   c. getting a recommendation from one of your former teachers
   d. researching a company and job position thoroughly before you have an interview

3. It is illegal for an interviewer to ask you about _____.
   a. your medical and mental health record
   b. your greatest weakness
   c. a time when you had to overcome an on-the-job challenge
   d. your computer skills

4. When the interviewer asks whether you have any questions, you should _____.
   a. say "no" so that it is clear you understood everything the interviewer said
   b. ask the interviewer a personal question in order to form a closer connection with him or her
   c. ask when you might be able to expect your first raise
   d. have one or two questions prepared that are tailored to the specific job or company

5. A _____ interview takes place early in the hiring process and helps employers narrow down the field of applicants.

    a. selection   **b.** screening   **c.** work-sample   **d.** group

6. When writing a thank-you note to the interviewer, you should _____.

    a. ask if there is someone higher up at the company that you can contact

    b. ask when the employer plans to make a hiring decision

    c. write a long note to show that you put in a lot of time and effort

    d. keep it simple, polite, and to the point

7. While waiting to hear back from the interviewer, it is a good idea to _____.

    a. call to follow up, even if the interviewer told you not to do so

    b. e-mail the interviewer daily to show your interest in the job

    c. research the general salary range for the position and prepare questions about benefits

    d. try to think of any mistakes you made during the interview

8. Benefit packages may include all of the following, except _____.

    a. health insurance   **c.** paid holidays and sick days

    b. raises   **d.** retirement plans

2 Positive and Negative. When confronted with any situation, we can respond in either a positive or negative way. Read the situations listed below, and then give an example of both a positive and a negative response. Study the example before you begin.

1. *Situation*: The bus on which you're riding to your job interview has just broken down, and you realize that you can't make it to the interview on time.

    Positive:

    Call the interviewer as quickly as possible, explain the circumstances causing the delay, and request another appointment.

    Negative:

    Think "Well, that's the story of my life," sit back, and feel sorry for yourself while the bus is being repaired.

2. *Situation*: It is the morning of an important job interview, and you are deciding what to wear.

    Positive:

    _____

    _____

    Negative:

    _____

    _____

3. *Situation*: At the beginning of the job interview, the interviewer asks you to describe what skills you have to offer.

Positive:

_____

_____

Negative:

_____

_____

4. *Situation*: You learn that someone else was hired for the job you were hoping to get.

Positive:

_____

_____

Negative:

_____

_____

3 Work with Classifications. Enter the following abbreviations under the correct classification on the chart below. Don't forget the necessary periods. Study the example before you begin.

✓AL	Fr.	Jap.	NY	Sat.
Aug.	Fri.	lb.	oz.	Sept.
CA	gal.	MA	pt.	Thurs.
Dec.	Ital.	Mar.	qt.	WA
Eng.	Jan.	Mon.	Rus.	Wed.

Days of the week	Languages	Measurements	U.S. States	Months of the year
			AL	

4 How Would You Classify This? Choose the word in the row that is the best classification for the first word, and write it on the blank line. Study the example before you begin.

1. **Alabama:**	city	state	nation	the South	**state**
2. **honesty:**	mood	quality	talent	emotion	
3. **salary:**	outcome	expense	income	benefits	
4. **co-worker:**	boss	job title	career	employee	
5. **ability:**	risk	honor	skill	duty	
6. **policy:**	illegal	rule	idea	choice	
7. **guarantee:**	promise	signature	experiment	preference	
8. **felony:**	crime	attitude	omission	punishment	
9. **paper:**	page	history	novel	material	
10. **social:**	habit	experience	personality	thought	
11. **Internet:**	technology	electronic	occupation	telecommute	
12. **respectful:**	duty	choice	manner	strategy	

5 More Work with the Suffix -ly. Choose the word that correctly completes each sentence, and write it in the blank. Study the example before you begin.

legal ✓legally	1. The landlady wondered whether or not she was **legally** responsible as she surveyed the minor water damage in the first-floor apartment.
positive positively	2. Eddie was _____ that after doing such a fine job mowing Mrs. Cash's lawn he would be given referrals for other jobs.
immediate immediately	3. Ginger's _____ availability was one reason she landed the job as a computer operator, a last-minute opening she read about in the Sunday classifieds.
fearless fearlessly	4. To work as a lion tamer, you must be able to perform your job _____.

current currently	**5.** "The applicant's file is _____ under review, and I should have an answer to your question by early next week," replied the Human Resources worker to her manager.
useless uselessly	**6.** "It's _____ for me to try to talk some sense into you," moaned the manager. "Since you're the owner of the team, you're going to do things the way you want to in spite of my excellent advice."
popular popularly	**7.** A compact disc is _____ known as a CD.
separate separately	**8.** Best friends Amrita and June applied _____, but they both got jobs at the same company.
impolite impolitely	**9.** It is _____ to ask co-workers what they earn.
useful usefully	**10.** The Internet can be a very _____ tool for researching careers.
social socially	**11.** Jeremy understood that _____ networking was very important, so he made sure to join several professional chat groups.
negative negatively	**12.** "I'm not speaking _____; I'm just being realistic," stated the barber who predicted that few customers would cross his doorway that Friday because of the eight-inch snowstorm the night before.
individual individually	**13.** Martin surrounded his birthday cake with _____ wrapped gifts for every guest he had invited to celebrate his fortieth birthday—a major event in his mind.
previous previously	**14.** Gail was _____ earning less than she is in her new job, which she got after improving her computer skills.
realistic realistically	**15.** "You can't _____ expect me to keep this silly curfew every weekend!" Dan's teenage daughter complained.

6 Filling out an Employment Application. For most jobs, you need to fill out an application before you are considered for an interview. Fill out the sample employment application on the following pages. Some of the words may be new to you, but if you sound them out according to rules you have studied previously, you should have no trouble. Use a dictionary to help you with the meanings.

EMPLOYMENT APPLICATION

PERSONAL

Name	Date:
Address	Phone Number:

City	State	Zip

Position applying for:	Date Available

Do you wish to work:
___ Full-time ___ Part-time

If part-time, hours or days:

Are you eligible to work in the United States?
___ yes ___ no

EDUCATION

	Name and Address of School	Dates		Did you Graduate?	Course or Degree
		From	To		
High School					
College or University					
Business or Trade School					
Other					

EMPLOYMENT INFORMATION

1.	Employer	Telephone	Dates Employed		Work Performed
			From	To	
	Address				
	Job Title		**Hourly Rate/Salary**		
	Immediate Supervisor		From	To	
	Reason for Leaving				
2.	Employer	Telephone	Dates Employed		Work Performed
			From	To	
	Address				
	Job Title		**Hourly Rate/Salary**		
	Immediate Supervisor		From	To	
	Reason for Leaving				

· **Attach resumé or separate piece of paper with additional job experience.**

Additional Training & Experience

Please indicate below the software programs in which you have experience or training.

_____

_____

_____

Please list any volunteer activities or awards related to this field of work.

_____

_____

_____

Do you belong to any professional organizations related to this field of work? ___ Yes ___ No   If so, explain.

_____

_____

_____

Have you been convicted of a felony or misdemeanor in the last 7 years? ___ Yes ___ No

---

REFERENCES

(Not Relatives) Please list three references (at least two professional references)

Name/Relationship	Occupation	Phone

Please Read Carefully:

I hereby state that these answers are correct and complete to the best of my knowledge and belief, and hereby permit the company to Investigate any of the information contained herein concerning my personal character, habits, or employment records. I understand that if I am hired, any false statement or omission of facts contained herein will be cause for my immediate dismissal. I understand this application is not a guarantee of employment.

Signature: _____ Date: _____

This company does not discriminate on the basis of age, color, religion, creed, disability, marital status, veteran status, national origin, race, gender, physical (or mental) handicap, or sexual orientation. This company is an Equal Opportunity Employer.

Words for Study

solution	pure	resumed	barrel
whitewash	inspiration	consent	innocent
surveyed	presently	reckon	victims
spirit	scorn	Polly	tadpoles
examined	artist	particular	idle

LESSON 10
How to Avoid a Job

by Mark Twain

Sometimes, as we all know, we just don't feel like working. In the passage below from Mark Twain's story *The Adventures of Tom Sawyer*, Tom hits upon a solution to this well-known problem.

* * *

Saturday morning was come, and all the summer world was bright and fresh and brimming with life. There was a song in every heart and cheer in every face. Tom appeared on the sidewalk with a bucket of whitewash and a long-handled brush. He surveyed the fence, and all gladness left him and a deep sadness settled down upon his spirit. Thirty yards of board nine feet high! Life to him seemed hollow and a burden.

Sighing, he dipped his brush and passed it along the topmost plank; repeated the operation; did it again; compared the white-washed streak with the vastness of unwhitewashed fence, and sat down on a box discouraged. He began to think of the fun he had planned for the day, and his sorrows multiplied. Soon, the free boys would come along, and they would make a world of fun of him for having to work—the very thought of it burnt him like fire. He got out his worldly wealth from his pocket and examined it—bits of toys, marbles, and trash; enough to buy an exchange of work maybe, but not half enough to buy so much as half an hour of pure freedom. So he gave up the idea of trying to buy the boys.

At this dark and hopeless moment, an inspiration burst upon him! Nothing less than a great, wonderful inspiration.

He took up his brush and went calmly to work. Ben Rogers came into sight presently—the very boy, of all boys, whose scorn he had been dreading. Ben was eating an apple and as he drew near, he slowed down and took to the middle of the street, playing a game in which he pretended he was a steamboat.

Tom went on whitewashing—paid no attention to the steamboat. Ben stared a moment and then said: Hi! You're up a stump, ain't you!

No answer. Tom surveyed his last touch with the eye of an artist; then gave his brush another gentle sweep and surveyed the result, as before. Ben ranged up alongside of him. Tom's mouth watered for the apple, but he stuck to his work.

Ben said, "Hello, old chap, you got to work, hey?"

Tom wheeled suddenly and said, "Why it's you, Ben! I warn't noticing."

"Say—I'm going in a-swimming, I am. Don't you wish you could? But of course you'd druther work—wouldn't you? Course you would!"

Tom studied the boy a bit and said, "What do you call work?"

"Why, ain't *that* work?"

Tom resumed his whitewashing and answered carelessly, "Well, maybe it is, and maybe it ain't. All I know is it suits Tom Sawyer."

"Oh, come now, you don't mean to let on that you *like* it?"

The brush continued to move.

Presently Ben said, "Say, Tom, let me whitewash a little."

Tom considered, was about to consent, but he altered his mind. "No—no—I reckon it wouldn't hardly do, Ben. You see, Aunt Polly's awful particular about this fence—right here on the street, you know—but if it was the back fence I wouldn't mind and *she* wouldn't. Yes, she's awful particular

about this fence; it's got to be done very careful; I reckon there ain't one boy in a thousand, maybe two thousand, that can do it the way it's got to be done."

"Oh, shucks, I'll be just as careful. Now lemme try. Say—I'll give you the core of my apple. I'll give you all of it!"

Tom gave up the brush with unwillingness written on his face, but with joy in his heart. And while Ben worked and sweated in the sun, the retired artist sat on a barrel in the shade close by, munched on his apple and planned the slaughter of more innocent boys. There was no lack of victims; boys happened along every little while; they came to jeer, but remained to whitewash. By the time Ben was tired, Tom had traded the next chance to Billy Fisher for a kite. And so on and so on, hour after hour.

When the middle of the afternoon came, Tom was rolling in wealth. For granting the honor of whitewashing, Tom had received in return twelve marbles, part of a Jew's harp, a piece of blue glass to look through, a key that wouldn't unlock anything, a piece of chalk, a tin soldier, a couple of tadpoles, six firecrackers, a kitten with only one eye, a brass doorknob, the handle of a knife, and four pieces of orange peel.

He had had a nice, good, idle time all the while—plenty of company—and the fence had three coats of whitewash on it! Tom said to himself that it was not such a hollow world, after all. He had discovered a great law of human action without knowing it—namely, that in order to make a man or a boy want something badly, it is only necessary to make the thing difficult to get. If he had been a great and wise man, he would have now understood that Work consists of what a body has to do, and that Play consists of whatever a body doesn't have to do.

1 About the Story. Answer the following questions in good sentence form.

1. At the beginning of the story, why does life seem "hollow and a burden" to Tom?

   _____

   _____

2. At the end of the story, why does Tom say to himself that the world is not so hollow after all?

   _____

   _____

3. Why was it probably a good thing for Tom that the first boy who came along was the boy "whose scorn he had been dreading"?

   _____

   _____

4. Why doesn't Tom let Ben whitewash the fence immediately after Ben says he'd like to try it?

   _____

   _____

5. What is the "law of human action" that Tom has used, without even realizing it, to get the boys to whitewash the fence for him?

   _____

   _____

6. According to Mark Twain, what is the difference between work and play?

   _____

   _____

7. Give an example of something that is work to you but might be considered play by someone else. Explain your reason for choosing this particular example.

   _____

   _____

8. Give an example of something that is play to you but might be considered work by someone else. Explain your reason for choosing this particular example.

   _____

   _____

2 If Only Someone Else Would Do It! Unlike Tom Sawyer, most workers can't go around tricking other people into doing their jobs. But if they could… Match the workers with the statements they might make to snare an innocent listener into taking their job for a day.

| butcher | dressmaker | lifeguard | stationmaster | teacher |
| cowboy | floorwalker | scribe | student | treasurer |

_____ 1. "Creating new patterns and ripping out seams is such a breeze that it's like being paid for relaxing."

_____ 2. "Doing homework is much more inspiring than hanging out with friends every evening."

_____ 3. "Grading homework is so much less demanding than doing it, and it's such a rewarding way to spend one's time."

_____ 4. "Nabbing shoplifters makes me feel just as brave and brainy as all those detectives you see on television."

_____ 5. "Nothing ever really bothers me because I know if things start to get frantic, I can always escape on the next train."

_____ 6. "Quartering these steers gives me all the muscles, money, and merriment that a man could ever hope for in life."

_____ 7. "Rescuing little children, getting a beautiful tan, flirting—that pretty well describes my ideal job."

_____ 8. "The greatest thing about handling the company's money all day is that I can pretend that it's mine and that I am rich."

_____ 9. "Riding herd on the range all day gives a body freedom and that feeling of being out where no boss can roam."

_____ 10. "Writing love letters for other people is far more exciting and less troublesome than actually being in love yourself."

Of these ten statements, which one sounds like something you'd like to do?

_____

_____

Which one sounds like something you'd never want to do?

_____

_____

3 Word Relationships. On the line, write the letter of the answer that best completes each statement. Study the example before you begin.

1. View is to sight as __*b*__.
    a. heat is to touch
    b. food is to taste
    c. scene is to sound
    d. stuffy nose is to smell

2. Major is to minor as _____.
    a. blameless is to innocent
    b. graduate is to enroll
    c. insecure is to worried
    d. vast is to immense

3. Fiber is to whole wheat bread as _____.
    a. vitamin C is to oranges
    b. vitamin D is to oranges
    c. calcium is to fruit
    d. protein is to vegetables

4. Examine is to investigate as _____.
    a. indicate is to reckon
    b. advice is to advise
    c. benefit is to aid
    d. resume is to dismiss

5. White is to wedding as _____.
    a. red is to wine
    b. green is to grass
    c. blue is to ocean
    d. black is to funeral

6. Italy is to Europe as _____.
    a. Egypt is to Asia
    b. Spain is to Africa
    c. Mexico is to South America
    d. Canada is to North America

7. Sextuplet is to six as _____.
    a. twin is to three
    b. octuplet is to eight
    c. trio is to three
    d. quintuplet is to seven

8. Medicine is to physician as _____.
    a. future is to ancestor
    b. diet is to weightlifter
    c. law is to judge
    d. cowboy is to gunfighter

9. Busybody is to nosiness as _____.
    a. consumer is to grouchiness
    b. hitchhiker is to fussiness
    c. volunteer is to unwillingness
    d. wallflower is to shyness

10. Vaguely is to precisely as _____.
    a. cheerily is to moodily
    b. immediately is to promptly
    c. positively is to certainly
    d. regretfully is to sorrowfully

4 Review of Suffixes. Add one of the suffixes listed in the box to the underlined word in each sentence so that the sentences make sense. When adding a suffix, you may need to drop or change some letters. Study the example before you begin.

| -ful | -less | -ly | -ment | -ness |

1. When the shortstop was thrown out of the game, he shouted at the umpire, "Your judge **ment** is as lousy as your eyesight!"

2. After a roast beef dinner and two servings of chocolate fudge cake, Grandfather lay down for his Sunday afternoon nap with a look of perfect content_____ on his face.

3. Although all wars could be described as senseless, World War II has been called "the most mercy_____ of all the wars."

4. Kenneth could tell by the blank_____ of his girlfriend's expression that she wasn't listening to a word he said.

5. "I'm delighted to report," said the nurse to the worried parents, "that your daughter's condition has vast_____ improved, and she will probably be moved to the children's ward after the doctor checks her chart."

6. It was pure_____ by accident, the young lovers thought, that fog had grounded the plane thus giving them a few more wonderful hours to spend with each other.

7. Mrs. Olson's arguments always turned into out-and-out battles because when she cast scorn_____ looks at all those who happened to disagree with her, they felt as if they had to defend their lives as well as their viewpoints.

8. Patty's tone of voice sounded innocent enough, but her mother knew from the vague_____ of her answers that she had been doing something she shouldn't have.

9. "Please be mercy_____ with this poor young man," pleaded the lawyer before the jury. "If you convict him, it is you who will be guilty of committing a crime."

10. Rob tried to be a duty_____ son, but it seemed as if his parents expected more of him than he was able to give.

11. Upon entering the two-room apartment, the caseworker immediately realized from the bare_____ of the front room that the family truly needed help.

12. "We didn't do it, ma'am," declared the leader of the gang innocent_____ when the policewoman demanded to know who had picked all the prize-winning roses in Mr. Frank's garden.

13. When Mr. Campbell heard that job opportunities in Alaska were limit_____, he decided he'd give moving there a try even though he wasn't particularly fond of freezing temperatures.

14. When the interviewer asked the couple how many children they had, Kirk shook his head and said sorrowfully, "None. My wife and I are child_____."

15. "Your misjudge_____ in this real estate deal has cost our firm thousands of dollars and you, your job. You're fired!" shrieked Ms. Shark to the shaking employee.

5 Spelling. Below are statements made by Mark Twain in some of his other books. One of the underlined words in each statement is misspelled. Rewrite the misspelled word correctly on the line.

_____ 1. One of the most <u>striking</u> <u>diffrences</u> between a cat and a lie is that a cat has <u>only</u> nine <u>lives</u>.

_____ 2. <u>Thunder</u> is good, it makes an <u>impression</u>: but it is <u>lightening</u> that <u>does</u> the work.

_____ 3. Each <u>person</u> is born to one <u>posession</u> which outvalues all his <u>others</u>—his last <u>breath</u>.

_____ 4. <u>Sorrow</u> can take care of <u>itself</u>, but to get the full <u>value</u> of a joy, you must have <u>sombody</u> to share it with.

_____ 5. "<u>Behold</u>," the fool says, "put not all <u>you're</u> eggs in one basket," but the wise man says, "put all your eggs in one basket and <u>WATCH</u> THAT BASKET."

_____ 6. If you pick up a <u>starveing</u> dog and make him <u>wealthy</u>, he will not bite you. This is the main <u>difference</u> <u>between</u> a dog and a man.

_____ 7. <u>April 1</u>. This is the day upon <u>which</u> we are reminded of what we are on the other three <u>hunderd</u> and <u>sixty-four</u>.

_____ 8. He is <u>useless</u>, on top of the ground; he ought to be under it, <u>inspiring</u> <u>cabages</u>.

_____ 9. It is <u>often</u> the case that the man who <u>cant</u> tell a <u>lie</u> thinks he is the best <u>judge</u> of one.

_____ 10. To <u>promis</u> not to do a thing is the <u>surest</u> way in the world to make a <u>body</u> want to go and do that <u>very</u> thing.

_____ 11. Let us be <u>thankfull</u> for the <u>fools</u>. But for them the rest of us <u>could</u> not <u>succeed</u>.

_____ 12. We should be <u>careful</u> to get out of an <u>expereince</u> only the <u>wisdom</u> that is in it—and stop there; lest we be like the cat that sits down on a hot stove lid. She will never sit down on a hot stove lid again—and that is well; but also she will never sit down on a cold one <u>anymore</u>.

6 What Exactly Is a Jew's harp? To learn more about this instrument, choose the correct word for each of the blanks in this description.

Asia	create	Europe	glory	popular
concerts	damaged	finger	incorrectly	resume
consists	dentist	gentlemen	instrument	traveled

The Jew's Harp

A jew's harp is not a harp. Neither is it, as some people _____ believe, a Jewish instrument. The jew's harp is a small musical instrument. It _____ of a curved metal frame with a metal strip connected to one end. The other end of the strip is slimmer and bent forward. Players hold the metal frame against their teeth and _____ musical notes by striking the metal strip with the _____.

Sometimes there are risks. In the early 1800s, for example, one performer who _____ throughout Europe giving _____ on the jew's harp had teeth that were so badly _____ by the iron instrument that he was in great pain every time he performed. He decided he had to start playing another instrument. But then, he found a _____ who agreed to construct a cover for his teeth. Using this cover, the performer was able to _____ playing his favorite _____.

The jew's harp has been played in Asia since the 1100s and in _____ since the 1300s. After a brief moment of _____ in the early 1800s, the jew's harp was replaced by the increasingly popular mouth organ. Currently, jew's harp playing is _____ in folk music and with children in the United States. And in _____, ladies are still courted by _____ playing quiet and romantic songs on this instrument.

1 Word Review. Use the words listed below to fill in the blanks correctly. Don't forget to capitalize when necessary.

Abraham Lincoln	experiment	Mark Twain	suffix
applicant	felony	prefix	United Nations
crisis	interview	roll call	whitewash

_____ 1. a face-to-face meeting for the formal discussion of some matter; a talk between a reporter and a person from whom he seeks facts or statements

_____ 2. a letter or letters added to the end of a word to alter its meaning or form a new word

_____ 3. a letter or letters put before a word that alters its meaning

_____ 4. a mixture of lime and water, often with glue added, that is used to whiten walls, concrete, etc.

_____ 5. a serious condition in which a sudden or meaningful change seems about to occur; an extremely important moment or situation; a turning point

_____ 6. a test made to decide the value of something previously untried, prove a known truth, or examine an idea

_____ 7. American author (1835–1910) who wrote *The Adventures of Tom Sawyer*

_____ 8. an organization of countries with headquarters in New York City which was founded in 1945 to promote world peace and security

_____ 9. any of several crimes such as murder, rape, or burglary which can result in strict punishment

_____ 10. one who applies for something, such as a job

_____ 11. the reading aloud of a list of names of people, as in a classroom or military post, to see who is absent

_____ 12. sixteenth president of the United States who served as president during the War Between the States (1861–1865)

2 Word Review. Write the letter of the word that could best replace each underlined word or phrase in the blank on the left.

_____ 1. After a long discussion, the employees at the travel agency decided upon a stagecoach for their <u>sign</u> because it suggested trips filled with adventure and excitement.
   a. application   **b.** judgment   **c.** quality   **d.** symbol

_____ 2. After the interview, Ralph had the <u>feeling</u> that he should have said more about his previous job experience.
   a. admission   **b.** commission   **c.** impression   **d.** omission

_____ 3. "Don't worry," said Dr. Ruby, "a few <u>slight</u> adjustments, and your back will feel just fine again."
   a. minor   **b.** major   **c.** pure   **d.** unpleasant

_____ 4. Francis <u>turned up his nose at</u> the salary offer because he thought he was worth far more than the petty sum the interviewer had just quoted.
   a. adjusted   **b.** preferred   **c.** reckoned   **d.** scorned

_____ 5. From sunrise to sunset, Peggy preferred to have every moment of her day completely planned because <u>idle</u> periods of time always made her feel uneasy and tense.
   a. undesirable   **b.** unstructured   **c.** unusual   **d.** unworthy

_____ 6. The chairman argued that Hiram should be put in charge of the fund-raising drive because he was <u>somebody you could always count on</u> when it came to hard work.
   a. available   **b.** dependable   **c.** forceful   **d.** realistic

_____ 7. The commander inspired such <u>intense</u> loyalty among his troops that they probably would have followed him anywhere.
   a. fierce   **b.** individual   **c.** lifelong   **d.** merciless

_____ 8. The jogger gave the policewoman his viewpoint of how the accident had happened and then <u>continued</u> jogging.
   a. advised   **b.** experienced   **c.** resumed   **d.** undertook

_____ 9. There was such <u>a warmth of feeling</u> in the way the host greeted his guests that Jane was glad she had accepted the invitation to his party.
   a. awareness   **b.** politeness   **c.** heartiness   **d.** seriousness

_____ 10. When the man in front of her at the checkout counter lit a cigar, Mrs. Stern tapped him lightly on the shoulder and <u>pointed to</u> the No Smoking sign hanging from the magazine rack.
   a. indicated   **b.** advertised   **c.** promoted   **d.** surveyed

_____ **11.** When the reporter asked the composer how he had created such a beautiful piece of music, he replied, "It was <u>a wonderful idea</u> followed by a lot of hard work."

    a. impression   **b.** information   **c.** innocence   **d.** inspiration

_____ **12.** When Peter ate in a restaurant, he was never very <u>fussy</u> about the food so long as the service was polite and prompt.

    a. particular   **b.** impolite   **c.** questioning   **d.** regretful

3 Review of Capitalization Rules. Write five sentences that show that you have an understanding of at least *ten* of the fourteen rules you have studied. To help you recall the rules, they are listed below. Note that the example uses five of these rules.

Review of Capitalization Rules

1. Capitalize the first letter of the first word in a sentence.

2. Capitalize people's names.

3. Capitalize the word *I*.

4. Capitalize calendar items. Do not capitalize seasons.

5. Capitalize place names.

6. Capitalize the names of races, nationalities, and languages.

7. Capitalize special events.

8. Capitalize historical events and periods in history.

9. Capitalize names of business firms and brand names of business products.

10. Capitalize the names of organizations.

11. Capitalize the first word and all important words in titles of books, plays, movies, magazines, newspapers, stories, poems, works of art, and pieces of music.

12. Capitalize names referring to the one God of a religion, religions and their followers, and major religious writings. Do not capitalize the word *god* when it is used to refer to a religion with many gods.

13. Capitalize language courses and course names followed by a number. Do not capitalize the names of school subjects.

14. Capitalize East, West, North, and South when they refer to recognized sections of the country or of the world. Do not capitalize these words when they tell directions.

Example:

 When Mrs. Jackson left Joe's Meat Market, she couldn't remember whether she
 had parked her Ford on Hillside Avenue or Baker Street.

1. _____

   _____

   _____

2. _____

   _____

   _____

3. _____

   _____

   _____

4. _____

   _____

   _____

5. _____

   _____

   _____

4 Looking for a Job. Use these classified advertisements to help you answer the questions which follow.

BABY SITTER NEEDED, in my own home. 3 children, hrs. 3p.m.–6p.m. Mon–Fri. Refs a must. Own transp. 555-0213 between 10a.m.–8p.m.	**DRIVER** Earn extra cash after work or school. Need a warm. resp. person to pick up children after school & drive to lessons, etc. 3–4 days per week. Own car nec. Call 555-0117.	**RESTAURANT HELP WANTED.** Kitchen help, bus people, waiters & waitresses, lunch & dinner shift. Please apply in person between 3–15p.m. Mon–Fri, Cider Barrel Restaurant.	**TIRE CHANGER.** Experience preferred, but will train. Benefits, good salary. Call 555-4042 for appointment.
BAR STAFF, WAITRESS & PORTER Full and part time. Starting week of 9–3. No phone calls please. Brookfield Bowling Center.	**OFFICE CLERKS.** Full time 9a.m.–5p.m. & 4p.m.–11p.m. High School Graduate with at least 6 months office experience. Newtown area. Call 555-2574, between 11a.m. & 3p.m.	**SALES HELP FOR CRAFT STORE,** Part time 10a.m.–5p.m. 3 days per wk. Craft experience pref. but not necessary. Call 555-1776	**TRUCK DRIVER,** Must have class II Driver's license and be 21 years of age or older, 1st & 2nd shifts open. Call 555-2931 between 8a.m. & 5p.m.
BARTENDERS, Waiters. Waitresses. Bus People. We are now hiring at Gregory's Restaurant Experience necessary. Apply in person: 265 Federal Rd., Brookfield bet. 2–4	**PAINTER**-If you have 5 yrs. experience as a painter and are making less than $9 an hr. Call after 5p.m. 555-5622.	**SALES PERSON**-full time, Mon. thru Fri. 9a.m–5:30p.m. Apply in person: English Drug. 140 South Ave.	**TYPIST** – Part time. 20 hrs. wk. Answer phones, general office duties Call 555-2333
CHEF'S ASSISTANT experience preferred. Salary dependent upon experience. Immediate opening for hard working, creative individual Call 555-2567	**PET SHOP CLERK** Part Time 9a.m.–1p.m. Call for appt 555-3141	**SALES-WEEKENDS PET SHOP.** Must know birds and fish, more days avail. 555-2747.	**WAITERS-WAITRESSES.** Full and part time, all shifts available. Opportunity for advancement. Apply: Fiddler's Lodge
CHILD CARE-Before school care needed for 2 children. 3 mornings wkly. Excel. pay. Call 555-2011	**PHOTO STORE**-Space Lab 1 Hour Foto now hiring. Full & part time positions available. Exper. helpful but will train. Call 555-3515	**SERVICE AGENT POSITION**-Part time for major car rental co. in Danbury. Responsibilities are servicing cars for rental. Weekends a must. Good pay and benefits. 555-5450 EOE m-f.	**WAREHOUSE**-Full time. We are in need of shipping, receiving and stock clerks, no exper. needed. Driver's lic. and a little knowledge of math needed. Call Mon–Fri. 9 a.m.–4 p.m., for application and interview: 555-8174.
CLEANERS—we have part time positions available, job inclds. wash day and folding of laundry. some counter work. Hrs. Sat. 8–4:30p.m., or Wkdays 2p.m.–6p.m. Call 555-7600 for more info.	**PRESSER** needed for shirt unit. Full time Tuesday–Saturday. $250–$350 per wk. depending on ability. Must be dependable. No experience necessary. Call Easy Cleaners. 555-1497	**TELEPHONE SALES** 25 hrs pr wk. day or evening hours Hourly plus commission. Phone 555-7355	**WAREHOUSE**-Full time. We are in need of shipping, receiving and stock clerks, no exper. needed. Driver's lic. and a little knowledge of math needed. Call Mon–Fri. 9 a.m.–4 p.m., for application and interview: 555-8174.
CONTROL DESK PERSON a.m., p.m. & weekends. No phone calls please. True Roll Bowling Lanes. 200 Federal Rd., Lancaster.		**TELEPHONE SALES & APPOINTMENTS,** 10 immediate positions Part time mornings or evenings. No experience required. Call 555-0104. E.O.E.	

1. What do the following abbreviations stand for?

   a. refs. _____

   b. transp. _____

   c. wkly. _____

   d. resp. _____

   e. pref. _____

   f. avail. _____

   g. co. _____

   h. lic. _____

2. Which two numbers would you call if you enjoy working with animals?

   _____ and _____

3. What does "hourly plus commission" mean in the TELEPHONE SALES ad?

   _____

4. Name one ad you would respond to if you only wished to work part-time.

   _____

5. Name one ad you would not respond to if you wanted to have your weekends free.

   _____

6. What is E.O.E. an abbreviation for in the TELEPHONE SALES & APPOINTMENTS ad?

   _____

What do you think? Which job looks the best to you? What do you like about it? Is there anything you don't like about it?

_____

_____

_____

_____

_____

_____

5 Find the Quote. Can you find this quote about work?

A. Each of the twelve descriptions defines or gives a clue for a certain word. Write that word on the lines to the left of each description.

B. Put the letters of these words in the blanks at the end of this section. The quote, when all the blanks are filled in, will be a thought about working.

C. The first one has been done for you. Study it before you begin.

P E N K N I F E
13 44 20 29 5 47 34 18

___ ___ ___   ___ ___ ___ ___ ___   ___ ___ ___
61 80 76   25 59 27 75 48   3 73 18

___ ___ ___ ___ ___ ___ ___ ___
65 4 48 10 53 67 22 43

___ ___ ___ ___ ___ ___ ___ ___ ___
8 63 40 79 14 49 53 6 21

___ ___ ___ ___ ___ ___ ___ ___
2 45 70 72 39 60 28 60

___ ___ ___ ___ ___ ___ ___ ___
53 9 37 58 1 35 14 61

___ ___ ___ ___ ___ ___ ___ ___ ___ ___
6 19 12 54 1 50 15 60 48 35

___ ___ ___ ___ ___ ___ ___
52 69 81 16 30 38 23

___ ___ ___ ___ ___
68 57 62 71 56

___ ___ ___ ___ ___ ___
66 42 53 55 78 7

___ ___ ___ ___ ___ ___ ___ ___
74 11 41 33 46 80 14 24

___ ___ ___ ___ ___ ___ ___ ___ ___ ___
36 51 6 32 31 17 77 26 44 64

1. another name for a small pocketknife

2. the holiday celebrated on December 31st (3 words)

3. the antonym of negative

4. this whistles when the water is boiling

5. the capital of Hawaii

6. considered an unlucky number by many people

7. a tall structure topped by a powerful light used as a signal to aid ships

8. an early stage of a frog or toad

9. Mommy's partner

10. what carries blood away from the heart to all parts of the body

11. the person who operates the train and waves to people from his cab

12. a person, usually a woman, who doesn't enter into the fun at a social event because she is shy or unpopular

Quote:

___ ___ ___   ___ N ___ ___   ___ ___ ___ ___ ___   ___ P ___ ___ ___ ___ E   ___ N
1   2   3   4   5   6   7   8   9   10   11   12   13   14   15   16   17   18   19   20

___ ___ ___ ___ ___   ___ ___ ___ K ___   ___ ___   ___ ___ F ___   ___ ___ ___ ___
21   22   23   24   25   26   27   28   29   30   31   32   33   34   35   36   37   38   39

___ ___ ___ E   ___ ___   ___ I ___   ___ ___ ___ ___   ___ ___ ___ ___
40   41   42   43   44   45   46   47   48   49   50   51   52   53   54   55   56

___ ___ ___   ___ ___ ___ ___ ___ ___ ___ ___   ___ ___ ___
57   58   59   60   61   62   63   64   65   66   67   68   69   70   71

___ ___ ___ ___ ___ ___ ___ ___ ___ ___ !
72   73   74   75   76   77   78   79   80   81

6 Compound Words. To complete these sentences correctly, choose a word from **List A** and add a word from **List B** to it. If necessary, use a dictionary to help you complete this exercise.

List A	List B
after	brain
air	case
check	cob
cook	front
corn	line
fiddle	long
hay	mate
life	out
master	piece
mouth	post
scatter	sick
sea	stack
side	sticks
sign	swiped
stair	taste
water	wash

1. Driving his tractor up and down the field in a vain search for his favorite _____ pipe which he had lost that morning, the farmer muttered, "This is like searching for a needle in a _____."

2. Karen was such a _____ that she forgot she hadn't taken her vacation trip to France yet and mindlessly threw away her _____ ticket while cleaning out her purse.

3. "Oh _____!" exclaimed a disappointed Aunt Polly when she heard the forecaster predict heavy thundershowers and realized their _____ would have to be called off.

4. Standing on the top step of the _____, Jimmy heard his wife declare, "_____!" from the den below, and was relieved that his wife had finally won the three-hour chess game, that his brother-in-law would finally go home, and that they could go to bed at last.

5. Stepping out the front door, Mr. Sutter's spirits sank to an all-time low when he discovered that some crazy fool had not only knocked over the _____ which advertised his carpentry business, but also had _____ his truck.

6. The four pieces of garlic bread Tim had eaten at the Madisons' housewarming party left an unpleasant _____ in his mouth that even gargling twice with _____ didn't help.

7. The workers on the _____ stopped unloading the ship for a moment to watch the _____ passengers from the *S. S. Dreamboat* stagger down the gangplank.

8. While putting the last touches on the painting, the artist rejoiced that he had finally succeeded in his _____ dream: to create a great _____.

Going Places

The English author Robert Louis Stevenson once wrote, "For my part, I travel not to go anywhere, but to go. I travel for travel's sake. The great affair is to move." Some people would not agree that traveling just for the sake of traveling is a good way to spend time. Most people, however, do enjoy being able to go places. In this unit, you will learn more about some people who have done—or tried to do—just that.

Mark Twain, the author of *The Adventures of Tom Sawyer*, is also the author of the reading for Lesson 11. Taken from his book *Life on the Mississippi*, this reading describes a disaster that occurred when a Mississippi River steamboat blew up.

Someone once said, "More than anything else, the automobile expresses the American desire to be on the go." In the reading for Lesson 12, "The Automobile Revolution," a respected American writer explores the effects the automobile has had on our way of life.

As we learn in "Caught in Traffic," traffic jams can be caused by things other than cars. In this short story, the reading for Lesson 13, we see what happened to two people caught in a traffic jam.

The reading in Lesson 14, "A Ride in Space," deals with a very different kind of travel. Sally Ride, the subject of this reading, was the first American woman to travel in space.

You will encounter still another kind of travel in Lesson 15. Just as the title suggests, this selection describes a strange trip from "New York to France—in a Rowboat."

Words for Study

captain	ruins	conscious	modern
aboard	accommodated	patients	provided
pilothouse	adrift	wad	compliments
chimneys	moor	chief	access
tragic	vessel	morphine	considerations
imprisoned	naked	attendants	Jacuzzi

LESSON 11
Life on the Mississippi
by Mark Twain

The reading selection below is taken from Mark Twain's book, *Life on the Mississippi*. In this selection, Twain describes a tragic steamboat accident that his brother was involved in. Twain, himself, was not on the boat. He was on another Mississippi steamboat and first learned of the accident when it pulled into a Mississippi town. But it was not until his boat reached Memphis, Tennessee, that he got the complete details. This is Twain's account of the accident.

* * *

It was six o'clock on a hot summer morning. The *Pennsylvania* was creeping along, north of Ship Island, about sixty miles below Memphis on a half-head of steam. The second mate had the watch on the deck. Most of the crew, including my brother Henry, were asleep. The captain was in the barber's chair, and the barber was preparing to shave him. There were a good many cabin passengers aboard, and three or four hundred deck passengers.

George was in the pilothouse—alone, I think—and he rang to "come ahead" full steam. The next moment four of the eight boilers exploded with a terrifying crash, and the whole forward third of the boat was hoisted toward the sky! The main part of

the mass, with the chimneys, dropped upon the boat again. And then, after a little while, fire broke out.

Many people were flung great distances and fell in the river, including my brother. Some of the crew were never seen or heard of again after the explosion. The barber's chair, with the Captain in it and unhurt, was left with everything forward of it, floor and all, gone. The stunned barber, who was also unhurt, stood with one toe projecting over space, still stirring his shaving cream and saying not a word.

By this time, the fire was beginning to threaten. Shrieks and groans filled the air. A great many persons had been scalded, a great many crippled; the explosion had driven an iron crowbar through one man's body. Both mates were badly scalded, but they stood their posts, nevertheless. They drew a wood boat near, and the captain fought back the frantic herd of frightened passengers till the wounded could be brought there and placed in safety first.

When Henry and another crew member fell in the water, they struck out for shore, which was only a few hundred yards away; but Henry believed he was not hurt (what a tragic error!) and decided to swim back to the boat and help save the wounded. So they parted, and Henry returned.

By this time the fire was making fierce headway, and several persons who were imprisoned under the ruins were begging for help. All efforts to put out the fire proved fruitless. One of the prisoners said he was not injured, but he could not free himself. When he saw that the fire was likely to drive away the workers, he begged that someone would shoot him, and thus save him from the more dreadful death. The fire did drive the axmen away, and they had to listen, helpless, to this poor fellow's pleas till the flames ended his pain.

The fire drove all that could be accommodated into the wood boat the mates had pulled up; the boat was then cut adrift, and it and the burning steamer floated down the river toward Ship Island. They managed to moor the wooden vessel at the head of the island, and there, unsheltered from the blazing sun, the half-naked survivors had to remain for the rest of the day without food or help for their hurts. Finally, a steamer came along and carried them to Memphis. By this time Henry was no longer conscious. The physicians examined his injuries, saw he would not survive, and turned their main attention to patients who could be saved.

Forty of the wounded were placed upon straw-filled beds in a public hall, and among these was Henry. There, the ladies of Memphis came every day with flowers, fruits, and other gifts, and there

they remained and nursed the wounded. All the physicians stood watches there, and all the medical students. The rest of the town furnished money or whatever else was wanted. Memphis knew how to do all these things well, for many a disaster like the *Pennsylvania's* had happened near her doors.

I watched there six days and nights, and a very sad experience it was. Two long rows of forms—and every face and head a shapeless wad of loose raw cotton. I saw many poor fellows removed to the "death room"—a room where the doomed were placed, so the others would not have to watch them actually die. The fated one was always carried out with as little stir as possible, and the stretcher was always hidden from sight. No matter: everybody knew exactly what was happening.

The chief mate was the only one who went to the death room and returned alive. His hurts were frightful, and he looked like nothing human. He was often out of his mind; and then his pains would make him carry on and shout and sometimes shriek. Now and then, he would tear off handfuls of the cotton and expose his cooked flesh to view. It was terrible.

The doctors tried to give him morphine to quiet him. But, in his mind or out of it, he would not take it. He said his wife had been killed by that drug, and he would die before he would take it. He was convinced that the doctors were concealing it in his medicine and in his water—so he ceased from putting either to his lips. Once, when he had been without water for two extremely hot days, he took the dipper, and the sight of the fluid and pain of his thirst tempted him almost beyond his strength; but he mastered himself and threw it away. After that he allowed no more water to be brought near him. Three times I saw him carried to the death room; but each time he revived, cursed his attendants, and demanded to be taken back. He lived to be mate of a steamboat again.

The main physician did all that sound judgment and trained skill could do for Henry; but, as the newspapers had said in the beginning, his hurts were past help. On the evening of the sixth day, his wandering mind busied itself with matters far away and his nerveless fingers picked at his blanket. His hour had struck; we bore him to the death room, poor boy.

1 About the Reading. If necessary, refer to the reading to answer the following questions correctly.

1. Cause and Effect. Match the effects in the box below with the causes in the sentences. Study the example before you begin.

he begged the others to shoot him.	he returned to help rescue the wounded.
he was able to work again as a mate on a steamboat.	Memphis knew how to respond to the accident.
✓the barber was stunned.	the captain was unhurt.
the chief mate refused both medicine and water.	patients for whom there was no hope were taken to the death room.
the physicians gave him less attention.	the wounded were taken to Memphis.

a. Because the explosion was so sudden and terrifying, __the barber was stunned.__

b. Because only a section of the barbershop blew up, _____

c. Because Henry believed he was unhurt, _____
_____

d. Because one of the trapped persons aboard the steamer realized the fire would soon reach him,
_____

e. Because another steamer came along, _____
_____

f. Because of the seriousness of Henry's injuries, _____
_____

g. Because steamboat disasters were not uncommon, _____
_____

h. Because the physicians did not wish to frighten the patients, _____
_____

i. Because of the way his wife had died, _____
_____

j. Because the chief mate recovered from his injuries, _____
_____

2. What do you think? Mark Twain says very little about the death of his brother. Offer a reason that might explain his unwillingness to talk in detail about Henry's death.

_____

_____

_____

_____

2 Idle Threats. Many threats are not idle, but the ones listed below provide a good way to review some common prefixes. Use the words listed at the left to complete each of these "idle" threats.

attend
contend
extend
intend

1. *What the wealthy aunt said to her selfish niece:*

"I don't care what you _____ to do this evening! I _____ that if you don't _____ yourself and _____ my wedding like any dutiful niece would, I shall cut you out of my will faster than you can say 'three million dollars'!"

interview
overview
preview
review

2. *What the governor said to his newest staff member:*

"Just to give you a _____ of what we're in for—if we don't _____ our monthly reports and try to form some kind of an _____ of our progress to date, we're going to look like a bunch of fools at the press _____!"

advise
devise
revise
supervise

3. *What the plant manager said to the foreman:*

"If you can't _____ a better system when you _____ this stupid plan tonight, I shall _____ the company to find someone else to _____ this important project!"

admit
commit
submit
transmit

4. *What the captain of the security guard said to the traitor:*

"If you don't _____ that you were about to _____ an act of treason in attempting to _____ a message to the enemy, I shall _____ a request to have your entire family brought in for questioning."

conserve
deserve
preserve
reserve

5. *What the young lady said to her boyfriend:*

"If you don't _____ good seats for the concert, you might as

well _____ gas and not even come over here that evening

because you don't _____ any more of my time, and nothing will

_____ this relationship!"

compose
dispose
expose
impose

6. *What the coach said to the soccer player:*

"I hate to _____ on you just before the game, but if you

don't _____ of the garbage in your locker immediately,

I shall _____ a note for the bulletin board and

_____ every one of your sloppy habits to the entire team!"

compress
depress
express
impress

7. *What the wife said to her husband, who was running for the city treasurer's seat in the*
November election:

"You say writing these speeches and talking to crowds _____

you, but I say if you don't _____ your ideas about tax reform

into much shorter statements and learn to _____ yourself in

a more interesting way, you're going to _____ the voters as

nothing but a long-winded bore!"

contract
detract
extract
subtract

8. *What the dentist said to a patient:*

"If you refuse me permission to _____ this rotten tooth, not

only will you _____ even more serious dental problems, but also

your diseased mouth will _____ from your overall appearance

and _____ years from your life!"

3 Traveling by Steamboat. Mississippi steamboat trips are still a popular form of adventure for many Americans. If you haven't been discouraged by the Mark Twain reading and if you have a few thousand dollars to spare, you might want to plan a steamboat trip on the Mississippi someday. For your information, some facts about modern-day steamboat travel have been listed below. Use this information to answer the questions that follow.

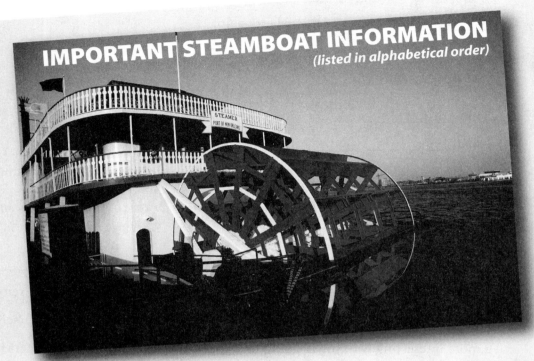

IMPORTANT STEAMBOAT INFORMATION
(listed in alphabetical order)

Air Conditioning: All vessels are fully air-conditioned.

Baggage: Baggage is not limited as long as it is in keeping with the length of the cruise. Properly mark your name and cabin number on your baggage tag. A porter will meet you at the gangway to take your baggage to your cabin.

Clothing: The Captain's Night dinner and the final night dinner are formal. Casual attire is recommended for the rest of the cruise.

Cruise Fares: Fares include transportation, cabin, meals, and onboard entertainment. Fares do not include personal items such as wine, photographs, gift shop purchases, or laundry.

Deck Chairs and Towels: These are provided compliments of the steamboat company.

Health Considerations: Doctors are not part of the boat's staff because of the nearness to shore and the many shore stops.

Insurance: It is suggested for your self-interest that you have insurance to cover anything that might occur during your trip. This service is available through insurance agents and most travel agents.

Jacuzzi: Located on the sun deck, the Jacuzzi is open year-round and heated to suit the temperature of the day.

Passage Contract: Passengers are to carefully review their passage ticket before boarding. This contract describes our legal relationship with you, and you will be asked to sign it upon boarding.

Personal Funds: Payment for onboard charges may be made by cash, personal check, traveler's checks, or credit card.

Pets: Pets of any kind are not permitted on board.

Third Persons: Third persons may share the cabin of two other full-fare passengers for an extra charge.

Wheelchair Access: There are two wheelchair-accessible cabins on board. Call for availability.

1. What do they call the rooms in which the passengers sleep on a steamboat?

   _____

2. Why would you probably pack a nice suit or dress if you were to go on this trip?

   _____

3. While on a steamboat, what would you do if you suddenly needed a doctor?

   _____

   _____

4. Whom do you contact to make sure you have the necessary insurance?

   _____

5. Why would a wheelchair-bound person need to call the steamboat company before making a reservation?

   _____

6. How much would you have to pay if you wanted to rent a deck chair?

   _____

7. On which deck is the Jacuzzi located? _____

8. Name an item you might purchase which is not included in your fare.

   _____

9. Why does the steamboat company advise you to read your ticket?

   _____

10. Do you think you would enjoy the steamboat company's cruise? Be sure to support your answer.

   _____

   _____

   _____

   _____

   _____

   _____

4 Synonyms and Antonyms. Choose a synonym to fill in the first blank in each sentence. Choose an antonym to fill in the second blank. Study the example before you begin.

Synonyms
abuse
active
compliment
faultless
formerly
✓moored
naked
offspring
precisely
ruin
seep
unending

Antonyms
✓adrift
ancestors
clothed
create
currently
gush
idle
incorrect
insult
passing
tenderness
vaguely

1. Secured and ___moored___ are antonyms for ___adrift___.

2. Bare and _____ are antonyms for _____.

3. Mistreatment and _____ are antonyms for _____.

4. Children and _____ are antonyms for _____.

5. Destroy and _____ are antonyms for _____.

6. Praise and _____ are antonyms for _____.

7. Lasting and _____ are antonyms for _____.

8. Exactly and _____ are antonyms for _____.

9. Trickle and _____ are antonyms for _____.

10. Errorless and _____ are antonyms for _____.

11. Previously and _____ are antonyms for _____.

12. Busy and _____ are antonyms for _____.

5 Contractions. A contraction is a shortened word formed by leaving out or combining some of the letters. Write the contractions for the following words. Study the examples before you begin.

1. is not ___isn't___
2. I am ___I'm___
3. do not _____
4. does not _____
5. did not _____
6. she is _____

7. it is _____
8. I would _____
9. I shall _____
10. he will _____
11. you are _____
12. you have _____

Words for Study

snobbishness	windshields	envy	hazard
plentiful	motorcycle	reckless	mph
revolution	popularity	criminals	absorbers
carriage	privacy	acids	sober
motorists	conflict	hitchhiker	yield

LESSON 12
The Automobile Revolution

by Frederick Lewis Allen

In 1906, a president of an American university stated that the automobile offered a picture of the snobbishness of wealth. Yet just less than twenty years later, an American housewife, in response to a comment on the fact that her family owned a car but no bathtub, uttered a fitting theme song for the automobile revolution: "Why, you can't go to town in a bathtub!"

When the automobile ceased to be a symbol of wealth for the few and became a need for the many, great changes in American life occurred. These changes, however, did not occur overnight. They could not. For they depended on three things. First, a car had to be made that the average American could afford, depend upon, and take care of without too much difficulty. Second, good roads had to be built. And third, garages and filling stations had to be plentiful. All these three requirements came slowly. A man who had tried to operate a filling station beside a dusty country road in 1906 would have speedily gone broke. It wasn't until the 1920s that the impact of the automobile revolution was felt most sharply from year to year.

When the university president spoke in 1906, and for years afterward, the automobile was a noisy thing that couldn't seem to make up its mind whether it was a machine or a horse-drawn carriage. Whenever you went for a drive—if you were wealthy enough to afford a car—you never knew just what to expect. Each car had a toolbox on the running board and motorists were used to carrying with them blowout patches, French chalk, and tire irons against the awful moment when a tire would pop miles from any help. The motorist had to crank the engine by hand—a difficult and sometimes dangerous business. Most cars were open, with windshields which gave only a minimum of protection against wind and dust to those in the back seat. Goggles were widely worn. Going for a ride in one of the early cars was much like riding on a motorcycle.

Then there was the problem of the roads. Roads were mostly dusty or muddy with no through routes. Even as late as 1921, there was no such thing as a numbered highway. In that year the *Automobile Blue Book* advised motorists to have a shovel with them for mountain roads, sandy stretches, and muddy places. In the early days of the automobile, horses were a danger for the driver, and speed limits set by country towns were sometimes low indeed. One American recalls that in a farming town in New Hampshire, the first legal limit was six miles an hour.

When Henry Ford was able to drive down the price of the automobile, automobiles became more popular. Equally responsible for the automobile's increasing popularity was a series of important improvements such as the invention of a self-starter in 1912. Perhaps the most important improvement was the introduction of the closed car. As late as 1916, only 2 percent of the cars made in the United States were closed; by 1926, 72 percent of them were. What had happened was that the automobile makers had learned to build closed cars that were not extremely expensive, did not rattle themselves to pieces, and could be painted with a fast-drying, lasting paint.

Meanwhile, the car-buying public discovered with delight that a closed car was something quite different from the old "horseless carriage." It was a power-driven, storm-proof room on wheels that could be locked and parked all day and all night in all weathers. You could use it to fetch home the groceries, cool off on hot evenings, reach a job many miles away, or visit distant friends. Young couples were quick to learn the privacy that this room on wheels gave them. Also, of course, the car often became a source of family conflict: "No, Junior, you are *not* taking the car tonight!"

Some people argued that the automobile destroyed the healthy habit of walking, weakened the churchgoing habit, promoted envy, killed innocent people when driven by reckless and drunken motorists, and provided criminals with a safe getaway. Nevertheless, the automobile was here to stay.

So it was that the years between 1918 and 1930 introduced to America a long series of new features which are now such a common part of the American scene that it is easy to imagine that they've always been around: traffic lights, concrete roads with banked curves, six-lane highways, motels, used-car lots, and roadside diners.

No such change in the habits of a nation could have taken place without having far-reaching social effects. Let us glance at a few of them:

1. The number of Americans whose home and place of employment were at least twenty miles apart vastly increased. As more and more people whose living was dependent upon work in the city fled to the outskirts for homes, city planners became concerned about the future of the city.

2. The automobile expanded Americans' sense of geography. One could still find, here and there, men and women who had never traveled farther

from home than the county seat, but their number was shrinking fast.

3. The automobile revolution brought sudden death. As cars became more powerful and roads became straighter and smoother, the number of people slaughtered yearly by cars in the United States increased. The shocking death toll led to more cautious licensing of drivers, the inspection of cars, an increased number of warning signs along the roadsides, and studies of the causes and cures of death on the highway.

4. The automobile age brought a parking problem that was forever being solved and then unsolving itself again. The question, "Where do I park?" is as annoying today as it has been at any time since the beginning of the automobile revolution.

5. The automobile revolution gave birth to a new kind of personal pride. The American might feel shame because he is poor, has an unimportant job, or by any other circumstance that might make him feel unworthy in his own eyes. But when he slides behind the wheel of an automobile, and it leaps forward at his command, this "unworthy soul" can imagine that he is truly "king of the road."

1 About the Reading. Put the letter of the correct answer in the blank.

1. The period which marked the greatest impact of the automobile on American life was _____.
   a. 1900–1910   **b.** 1905–1915   **c.** 1910–1920   **d.** 1920–1930

2. Henry Ford helped to make the automobile more popular when he _____.
   a. applied paint that would last to his cars   **c.** invented the self-starter
   b. constructed closed cars   **d.** made cars that people could afford

3. Based on the university president's statement in 1906, we can conclude that he _____.
   a. had little idea that the automobile would create such far-reaching changes in American life
   b. believed poor people shouldn't own automobiles
   c. had never had the pleasure of riding in an automobile
   d. was filled with envy because he couldn't afford a car

4. The early motorists wore goggles so they _____.
   a. could see the bumps and ruts in the road better
   b. would have some protection
   c. would look stylish
   d. would not be recognized by their friends

5. The group that seemed to be against the automobile in the early days was _____.
   a. criminals   **b.** housewives   **c.** farmers   **d.** young lovers

6. One reason cited by the author to explain the death toll on the highways is _____.
   a. the improvement of road conditions
   b. the lack of warning signs
   c. the number of people who worked in the city but no longer lived there
   d. the widespread use of cars by criminals

7. A driver who feels as if he is "king of the road" experiences _____.

   a. pride   **b.** greed   **c.** envy   **d.** royalty

8. Because of the Automobile Revolution, the number of _____ decreased.

   a. criminals   **b.** diners   **c.** homebodies   **d.** housewives

9. The author refers to the introduction of the automobile as the "Automobile Revolution" because _____.

   a. people gave up things they needed in order to buy a car

   b. poor people could now consider themselves as important as wealthy people

   c. so many changes occurred in the way Americans lived

   d. the American cities began to fall apart

10. The author's main reason for writing this passage seems to be _____.

    a. to argue the need for the American public to know more about the automobile

    b. to describe the viewpoints of those who thought the automobile was a terrible invention

    c. to explain the dangers introduced by the automobile

    d. to present the early history of the automobile

2 What Do You Think? In the early 1900s, few people imagined that the automobile would become a popular form of transportation. Using your imagination, describe what you think will be the most popular form of travel for people living one hundred years from now.

_____

_____

_____

_____

_____

_____

_____

3 More Work with Contractions. Write the contractions for the following words.

1. we would	_____		7. he is	_____
2. they would	_____		8. how is	_____
3. she will	_____		9. there is	_____
4. he will	_____		10. has not	_____
5. we are	_____		11. were not	_____
6. they have	_____		12. madam	_____

4 Word Relationships. For each of the following statements, choose the best answer, and write it on the line.

1. Earache is to painful as _____.
   a. disaster is to tragic
   b. purchase is to expensive
   c. revolution is to modern
   d. survivor is to unhurt

2. Plentiful is to scarce as _____.
   a. harsh is to serious
   b. long-winded is to talkative
   c. merciful is to forgetful
   d. taut is to slack

3. Razor is to barbershop as _____.
   a. attendant is to hospital
   b. dentist's office is to drill
   c. drill is to dentist's office
   d. hospital is to attendant

4. Abbreviate is to shorten as _____.
   a. alter is to revise
   b. clutch is to yield
   c. dismiss is to hire
   d. hassle is to supervise

5. Automobile is to motor as _____.
   a. bicycle is to handlebar
   b. carriage is to wheels
   c. jet is to pilot
   d. train is to engine

6. New Hampshire is to New England as _____.
   a. Michigan is to the East
   b. North Carolina is to the South
   c. Oklahoma is to the West
   d. Pennsylvania is to the Midwest

7. Expensive is to cheap as _____.
   a. devise is to provide
   b. extract is to remove
   c. positive is to imagined
   d. sober is to silly

8. "Fiddlesticks!" is to expression as _____.
   a. letters are to alphabetical order
   b. mph is to abbreviation
   c. she will is to contraction
   d. rules are to capitalization

9. Conserve is to waste as _____.
   a. bloom is to wilt
   b. redden is to blush
   c. submit is to reflect
   d. subtract is to multiply

10. Lifeboat is to steamer as _____.
    a. engineer is to train
    b. brakes are to bicycle
    c. passenger is to taxi
    d. airbag is to automobile

5 The Prefix *un-*. The most common prefix is *un-*, which means *not*. Use the words below to complete the sentences correctly.

undesirable	unfastened	ungrateful	uninterested	unlimited	unskilled
unexpected	unfruitful	uninformed	unleashed	unsafe	untrue

1. It is simply _____ that the automobile has had very little impact on how we live.

2. Blacksmiths found the popularity of the automobile particularly _____ because, in a few short years, they found themselves out of work.

3. Tommy was completely _____ in the fact that his sister needed a way to get home from play practice. All he knew was that it was his night to use the family car.

4. One reason that Americans are so _____ about the nation's transportation problems is that most newspapers confine their reporting of transportation issues to strikes and tragic accidents.

5. As Joe _____ his safety belt, he delicately rubbed his aching stomach and wondered if the extra money he was earning as a driving instructor was worth an ulcer.

6. Most attempts to improve the transportation system in the United States have been _____ because neither the city, state, nor federal governments have had a clear idea of what the goals should be.

7. Mrs. Wade was stunned when her husband presented her with a brand-new car for her fiftieth birthday; the gift was totally _____.

8. Of the 142 million tons of gases, soot, chemicals, and acids that are _____ into the skies of the United States each year, 82 million tons come from automobile, truck, and bus exhausts.

9. "A bunch of _____ boneheads must have worked on my car at that garage!" roared Mr. Valentine as his Volkswagen spluttered to a grinding halt in the middle of nowhere.

10. In the best-selling book, _____ *at Any Speed*, the description of how dangerous automobiles were finally prompted the federal government into forcing the automobile industry to make safer cars.

11. "You know, if you weren't so _____, people who give you lifts might be more willing to take you exactly where you want to go," the truck driver remarked after studying the look of resentment on the hitchhiker's face.

12. If everyone could drive at _____ speed, what do you think highway travel would be like?

6 Taking a Written Driver's Test. Here are some sample questions from the Connecticut driver's test. Circle the letter of the answer you think is correct. Then see how well you scored by comparing your responses with the answers that appear at the end of the test.

1. Your vehicle has a mechanical problem. What should you do?
   a. Signal and pull into the slow lane.
   b. Stop in your lane and put on your hazard lights.
   c. Put on your hazard lights and pull off the road.

2. At 50 mph, the distance required to stop a car is about:
   a. 1/4 block   b. 1/2 block   c. 3/4 block

3. Which of the following can cause problems when you're not moving?
   a. bad brakes   b. bad shock absorbers   c. bad exhaust system

4. You are driving in city traffic. How far ahead should you be looking?
   a. about 25 feet   b. about 1 block ahead   c. about 2 blocks ahead

5. To cross a stream of traffic in the city from a full stop, you need a gap of:
   a. 100 feet   b. 1/2 block   c. a full block

6. If you have had too much to drink, you can sober up by:
   a. drinking hot coffee   b. taking a cold shower   c. waiting several hours

7. When driving on a road covered with packed snow, you should reduce your speed by:
   a. 1/2   b. 1/3   c. 3/4

8. A traffic light with a flashing red signal means:
   a. Caution   b. Yield   c. Stop

9. If the rear of your car begins to skid sideways, you should:
   a. pump the brakes   b. apply the brakes gently   c. stay off the brake

10. If you are driving car 1, in which of the following pictures (A, B, or C) would it be most difficult to see car 2?

A	B	C
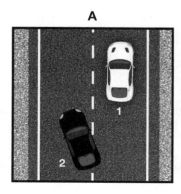	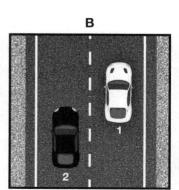	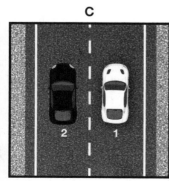

Answers: 1. c, 2. b, 3. c, 4. b, 5. b, 6. c, 7. a, 8. c, 9. c, 10. b

Words for Study

Anthony	gallop	devil	blindfolded
servant	vehicles	chapter	myth
generations	impatiently	rascal	Apollo
encyclopedia	reins	Cupid	weapons
society	Manhattan	mythology	apostrophe
Broadway	angel	pierces	contradicts

LESSON 13
Caught in Traffic

by O. Henry

Old Anthony Rockwall, who had made millions in the soap business and was now retired, looked out the library window of his Fifth Avenue mansion and grinned. "Mike!" he shouted to his servant in the voice he had used in his younger days on the Great Plains. "Tell my son to come in here before he leaves the house."

When young Rockwall entered the library, the old man looked at him with kindly seriousness. "You're a gentleman," said Anthony finally. "They say it takes three generations to make one, but they're wrong. Money will do it as slick as soap grease. It's made you one. By golly! It's almost made one of me."

"There are some things that money can't buy," remarked young Rockwall gloomily.

"Now, don't say that," said old Anthony, shocked. "I bet my money on money every time. I've been through the encyclopedia down to Y looking for something you can't buy with it."

"For one thing," answered Richard, "it won't buy one into the best circles of society."

"Ah," said Anthony keenly. "What's her name?"

Richard began to walk up and down the library floor.

"Why, she'll jump at you!" exclaimed Anthony. "You've got the money and the looks, and you're a decent boy. Your hands are clean. You've got no soap on 'em. You've been to college, but she'll overlook that."

"I'm too late. She's going to sail for Europe, I'm allowed to meet her with a cab tomorrow evening at Grand Central Station. We drive down Broadway at a gallop to Greenwood Theater, where her mother will be waiting for us in the lobby. Do you think she would listen to me tell her how much she means to me during those six or eight minutes under those circumstances? No, Dad, this is one tangle that your money can't unknot."

"All right, Richard, my boy," said old Anthony cheerfully. "You may run along now."

At eight o'clock the next evening, Richard's aunt took an old ring from a moth-eaten case and gave it to Richard. "Wear it tonight, nephew," she begged. "Your mother gave it to me. Good luck in love she said it brought. She asked me to give it to you when you had found the one you loved."

Young Richard took the ring and tried it on his smallest finger. It slipped as far as the second joint and stopped. He took it off and stuffed it into his vest pocket. And then he phoned for his cab.

At 8:32 that evening, Richard met his true love at Grand Central Station. "We mustn't keep Mother waiting," said she.

"To Greenwood Theater as fast as you can drive!" said Richard loyally.

The carriage whirled up Forty-second to Broadway. Then at Thirty-fourth Street, young Richard quickly thrust up the trap and ordered the driver to stop. "I've dropped a ring," he explained, as he climbed out. "It was my mother's, and I'd hate to lose it. I won't keep you a minute—I saw where it fell."

In less than a minute he was back in the cab with the ring.

But within that minute a cross-town car had stopped directly in front of the cab. The cabman tried to pass to the left, but a heavy express wagon cut him off. He tried the right, but had to back away from a furniture van that had no business being there. He tried to back out, but dropped his reins and swore dutifully. He was stuck in a tangled mess of horses and vehicles.

"Why don't we drive on?" said Richard's true love impatiently.

Richard stood up in the cab and looked around. He saw a flood of wagons, trucks, cabs, and vans filling the vast space where Broadway, Sixth Avenue, and Thirty-fourth Street cross one another. The entire traffic of Manhattan seemed to have jammed itself around them.

"I'm very sorry," said Richard as he resumed his seat, "but it looks as if we are stuck. They won't get this mess cleared for about an hour. It was my fault. If I hadn't dropped the ring we—"

"Let me see the ring," said the young lady. "Now that it can't be helped, I don't care. I think theaters are stupid anyway."

At eleven o'clock that night somebody tapped lightly on Anthony Rockwall's door.

"Come in," shouted Anthony, who was in a red dressing gown, reading a book about pirates.

Somebody was Richard's aunt, looking like a gray-haired angel that had been left on earth by mistake. "They're engaged, Anthony," she said softly. "She has promised to marry our Richard. On their way to the theater there was a traffic jam, and it was two hours before their cab could get out of it. And oh, Brother Anthony, don't ever boast of the power of money again. A little symbol of true love—a little ring—was the cause of our Richard's finding his happiness. What good could your money have done?"

"Sister," said Anthony Rockwall. "I've got my pirate into a devil of a scrape. His ship has just sunk, and he's too good a judge of the value of money to let it drown. I wish you would let me finish this chapter."

The story should end here. I wish it would as heartily as you who read it wish it did. But we must go to the bottom of the well for truth.

The next day a person with red hands and a blue necktie, who called himself Kelly, called at Anthony Rockwall's mansion and was at once received in the library.

"Well," said Anthony, "let's see—you had $5,000 in cash."

"I paid out $300 more of my own," said Kelly. "I had to go a little above our figure. I got the express wagons and cabs mostly for $5; but the trucks and two-horse teams mostly raised me to $10. The motormen wanted $10, and some of the loaded teams $20. The cops stuck me hardest—$50. But didn't it work beautiful, Mr. Rockwall?"

"Thirteen hundred—there you are, Kelly," said Anthony, tearing off a check. "Your thousand, and the $300 you were out. By the way," Anthony said to Kelly who was about to leave, "you didn't notice anywhere in the tie-up a kind of a fat boy without any clothes on shooting arrows around with a bow, did you?"

"Why, no," said Kelly, puzzled. "I didn't. If he was like you say, maybe the cops nabbed him before I got there."

"I thought the little rascal wouldn't be on hand," chuckled Anthony. "Good-bye, Kelly."

1 About the Story. Write the letter of the correct answer in the blank.

1. The setting of the story is _____.
   a. Chicago   **b.** Detroit   **c.** Los Angeles   **d.** New York

2. For which of the following does Anthony Rockwall seem to lack respect? _____.
   a. formal education   **b.** reading   **c.** Richard   **d.** money

3. When Anthony Rockwall tells his son his "hands are clean," he means _____.
   a. Richard bathes regularly   **c.** Richard is not a worker but a gentleman
   b. Richard is not a criminal   **d.** Richard has never been in love before

4. Richard's true love begins to relax after _____.
   a. Richard has asked her to marry him
   b. Richard has told her they are in a bad traffic jam
   c. Richard has met her at Grand Central Station
   d. the cross-town car has blocked their cab

5. Anthony Rockwall _____ his sister's claim that it was the ring that has brought Richard and his true love together.
   a. agrees with   **b.** disagrees with   **c.** ignores   **d.** scorns

6. From the aunt's statements, we can guess that Richard's mother _____.
   a. died from a broken heart   **c.** was responsible for her husband's success
   b. had died when Richard was a baby   **d.** was quite different from her husband

7. Whom did Kelly have the most trouble bribing? _____.

    a. the police   **b.** the motormen   **c.** the cabmen   **d.** the truck drivers

8. Who regrets that the story doesn't end before the scene in which Kelly pays a visit to the Rockwall mansion? _____.

    a. Anthony Rockwall   **b.** the author   **c.** Kelly   **d.** the cabmen

9. Although the story doesn't reveal the name of the "fat boy without any clothes on," who do you think he is? _____.

    a. Apollo   **b.** Bacchus   **c.** Cupid   **d.** Pan

10. If you had no idea what the answer to the last question was, you had company. Which character in the story has no idea who the "fat boy" is? _____.

    a. Kelly   **b.** Richard   **c.** Richard's aunt   **d.** Richard's love

2 The Apostrophe to Show Ownership. The punctuation mark you used to write contractions in Lessons 11 and 12 is called an *apostrophe*. An apostrophe is also used to show ownership. Below are two examples using the apostrophe to show ownership. Study them carefully. Then rewrite the remaining phrases in the same way.

1. the impression of Polly   Polly's impression

2. the uniform of the cheerleader   the cheerleader's uniform

3. the costume of the actress   _____

4. the effects of the morphine   _____

5. the coffee cake of Mrs. Mack   _____

6. the masterpiece of the screenwriter   _____

7. the wings of the angel   _____

8. the hives of the beekeeper   _____

9. the discovery of the chief   _____

10. the bad temper of Jackie   _____

11. the atmosphere of the earth   _____

12. the patients of the psychiatrist   _____

3 A Fat Boy without Any Clothes On. The "fat boy" to whom Anthony Rockwall referred in the story is Cupid. Use the words listed below to complete this passage about the Roman god of love.

arrows	deadly	pierces	sorry
bowstring	escape	plea	sprinted
create	eyes	prayed	supposed
crown	perched	reject	wildness

Cupid

In Roman mythology, Cupid is the god of love. He is often pictured as a chubby baby or child with wings who carries a bow and _____. With these arrows, he gaily _____ the hearts of men and women.

Sometimes Cupid is shown blindfolded to stress the _____ of his shooting. Also, some of his arrows were _____ to be tipped with gold to _____ strong love in his victims' hearts. The rest of his arrows—which had lead tips—caused his victims to _____ the love shown by others.

In one myth, Apollo, the Roman god of the sun, came upon Cupid, who was stringing his little bow. Apollo told him to leave the _____ weapons to grown-ups and play with toys instead. Smirking, Cupid continued to string his bow. When he was finished, he _____ on a ledge and took two arrows—one gold and one lead.

He put the lead arrow in his _____ and hit the heart of a lovely young maid. A moment later, he shot Apollo with the arrow of love just as Apollo's _____ fell upon the lovely young maid.

Certain that she would return his love, Apollo _____ after her. But the young maid tried to _____. When she realized that he was about to catch her, she _____ to her father, a river god, to save her. Her father answered her _____, and as Apollo reached her, she suddenly changed into a tree. Confused, he asked, "Why don't you like me?"

As the wind blew through the leaves, they answered, "I don't know." Then the tree felt _____ for Apollo and gave him a gift—a _____ of leaves that would never die. Apollo put the crown on his head and sadly went on his way. Cupid had won again!

4 More Prefixes That Mean *Not*. In addition to *un-*, five other prefixes can mean not: *il-*, *im-*, *in-*, *ir-*, and *non-*. Use the words below to complete the sentences correctly. Use each word only once.

illegal	improper	indecent	indigestion	inexperience	irresponsible	nonsense
impatient	impure	independent	indirect	insane	nonmetal	nonskid

1. When you drink _____ water, you may be in grave danger.

2. If you suffer from _____, you may be headed for an ulcer.

3. The selling of whiskey to minors is _____.

4. An _____ person cannot be depended upon.

5. Because of their _____, many new employees are given training programs by their employers.

6. Oxygen is an example of a _____.

7. An _____ state or country is one that is self-governing.

8. A person who speaks in an _____ way has trouble making himself understood.

9. The word _____ might be on your mind if you were shopping for a new set of tires.

10. _____ describes the clothing of a person who attends a formal wedding dressed in blue jeans, a sweat shirt, and sneakers.

11. _____ describes how a person would be regarded if he or she showed up at a formal wedding stark naked.

12. The actions of a madman can be described as _____.

13. You might reply, "_____!" when somebody tells you a story that you regard as silly or untrue.

14. If you have completed this exercise in an _____ manner, you may have made quite a few errors.

5 Money. Throughout the ages, much has been written about money. Put a check before the sayings cited below that might just as easily have been said by Anthony Rockwall.

_____ A fool and his money are soon parted.

_____ A lack of money is the root of all evil.

_____ How pleasant it is to have money!

_____ If a man is wise, he gets rich, and if he gets rich, he gets foolish, or his wife does. That's what keeps the money moving around.

_____ If making money is a slow process, losing it is quickly done.

_____ Make money, money by fair means if you can; if not, by any means.

_____ Money alone sets all the world in motion.

_____ Prefer to store money in the stomachs of the needy rather than hide it in a purse.

_____ Put not your trust in money, but put your money in trust.

_____ Remember that time is money.

_____ There are three faithful friends—an old wife, an old dog, and ready money.

_____ Though mothers and fathers give us life, it is money alone which preserves it.

Now choose any one of the sayings above, and describe an experience you've had that either supports or contradicts the saying.

_____

_____

_____

_____

_____

_____

_____

6 More about Money. When old Anthony Rockwall finished his pirate book, he might have enjoyed reading a poem like "The Rich Man" by Franklin P. Adams (1881–1960). After you've read the poem, answer the questions which follow.

The Rich Man

by Franklin P. Adams

The rich man has his motor-car,
    His country and his town estate.
He smokes a fifty-cent cigar
    And jeers at Fate.

He frivols through the livelong day,
    He knows not Poverty, her pinch.
His lot seems light, his heart seems gay;
    He has a cinch.

Yet though my lamp burns low and dim,
    Though I must slave for livelihood—
Think you that I would change with him?
    You bet I would!

1. What do you think *frivols* means in the first line of the second verse?

_____

2. Explain what *lot* means as it is used in the third line of the second verse.

_____

3. Does the poet seem to agree or disagree with old Anthony Rockwall's belief about money? Support your answer with examples from the poem.

_____

_____

4. Do you agree with the poet, or do you hold a different belief about money? Be sure to explain your thoughts in detail.

_____

_____

_____

_____

Words for Study

NASA	Soviet Union	assumed	retrieve
amnesia	cosmonaut	resourceful	announced
shuttle	parachute	assigned	satellite
launch	apron	designing	stow
orbiting	opinions	manipulator	cartoonist
capsule	radiator	remote	evidence

A Ride in Space

by Jerry Adler and Pam Abramson

In 1977, when Sally Ride was 25 years old and finishing up her studies at a California university, she spotted a notice in the school newspaper about openings in the astronaut program, a career that she had never even considered previously. She was up and out of the room before she had finished reading the notice, one of more than 1,000 women and nearly 7,000 men to apply for what would be the 35 slots in the astronaut class of 1978.

How NASA chose 35 people from the 8,000 applicants remains a mystery, although Ride's husband claims to have found one important key.

When asked by the NASA psychiatrist whether they had ever had amnesia, all the successful applicants seemed to have answered, "I don't know, I can't remember." Sally Ride must have given this response also, for she and five other women were among those accepted into NASA's class of 1978.

Six years later, on June 18, 1983, she and four other astronauts, all men, strapped themselves into seats on the flight deck of the space shuttle *Challenger* and, 44 minutes and 23.7 seconds after its thunderous launch, reached the final orbiting position beyond the fringe of the earth's atmosphere. This six-day mission was the seventh in the shuttle series and the second for the *Challenger*.

Thus, 22 years, 36 manned missions, and 57 astronauts after the first space capsule splashed into the Atlantic Ocean, Sally Ride became the first woman to wear the Stars and Stripes in space. Space itself is not expected to be changed much by the event, but it was surely an important moment for women. Ride herself stated to a reporter, "I did not come to NASA to make history. It's important to me that people don't think I was picked for the flight because I am a woman." Yet this was in fact one of the things NASA had in mind when Ride and the other women were accepted into the astronaut program. As a woman employee at the Johnson Space Center delicately explained, "At that time in our country, people were feeling a little bit bad about the way they had treated women."

Women had been in space before, although they had hardly left their mark on it. The first time was almost exactly 20 years before Sally Ride's flight aboard the *Challenger*. The woman was a 26-year-old factory worker and sky diver from Russia. She was launched aboard a rocket shortly before the Soviet Union was to serve as host to the World Congress of Women. The event attracted much public attention, although reports since then have held that the woman was sick for most of the three-day mission. Then, in August, 1982, in plenty of time to beat Ride's timetable, the Soviets launched their second woman cosmonaut, a 34-year-old test pilot and parachute ace. When her spacecraft docked with the orbiting Soviet space station, one of the two male cosmonauts manning the space station joked that he had an apron ready for her.

Like the Russians, Americans did not ignore the fact that Sally Ride is a woman. American newspaper and television reporters hounded Ride for her thoughts and opinions about being the first American woman in space and often complained that they were having trouble getting much information from her. Reporters demanded to know if Ride planned to wear a bra. "There is no sag in zero G," she explained. Reporters wanted to know if she cried when she had a problem. "Why doesn't someone ask the pilot of the shuttle mission those questions?" she responded with a smile. The pilot, of course, was a man.

Ride's answers to reporters were in keeping with her sister Karen's description of her: "Sally lives up to her own standards. What other people think of her

is not of the highest importance to her. She doesn't run around trying to make everyone happy, which most women tend to do."

In trying to describe some of the qualities that may have been responsible for Ride's success, Molly Tyson, her college roommate, recalled the time Sally's car broke down on a dark and deserted road, laid low by a burst radiator hose. Tyson assumed there was nothing to do but curl up in the back seat and wait for help to happen by. Ride, however, quickly created a repair with a roll of Scotch tape buried in the trunk, found a saucepan rattling around in back, and set off down the road in search of water, Within an hour they were back on the road. "I imagine she's going to be very resourceful up there in space," Tyson commented.

It was also one of the few times Tyson saw Ride pick up a saucepan. A government agent interviewed Tyson as part of a background check on Ride. "I only lied once," she recalled, "but I figured that dust and dirty dishes wouldn't collect in a space capsule the way they had in our apartment."

Tyson has also offered information about the Ride family, which she described as not at all your normal family: "They didn't have to sit at the same table for dinner. People ate dinner when they wanted, and they could have a whole dinner of nuts and cheese and crackers." In one sense, that was an ideal home for bringing up an astronaut; for Sally considers space food on the whole as "pretty good."

In Ride's first years with NASA, she was assigned to work on the team designing a manipulator arm for the shuttle, an engineering job that bore little relationship to her university training. Operated by remote control, the manipulator arm would send out and retrieve experiments. "I spent two years on it, and nothing else," Ride recalled. "As far as I knew, there was nothing else; what you did was launch an arm."

No one was surprised when the director of flight operations announced that Ride would be a member of STS-7, the second *Challenger* mission. The manipulator arm was first used on this mission. One of Ride's tasks during this space flight was to use the arm to snatch a 3,960 pound shuttle satellite floating in space and stow it in the cargo bay.

Ride has said that she doesn't plan to have children, which seems to have more to do with her feelings about raising children than it does with her career. Her father remembered that the first time Sally had a babysitting job, the children refused to eat the sandwiches she had made because she put the peanut butter and jelly in the wrong order. She threw the sandwiches out, made another batch, and never took another babysitting job again.

1 About the Reading. Put the letter of the best answer on the line.

1. What was most unusual about Ride's prompt response to the notice about openings in the astronaut program in her school newspaper? _____
   a. Her college background had not prepared her to become an astronaut.
   b. She had never even considered becoming an astronaut.
   c. She was applying for a man's job.
   d. She was twenty-five years old and hadn't yet finished school.

2. NASA's reason for accepting Sally Ride and her classmates in the astronaut program was _____.
   a. all of them had a good sense of humor
   b. none of them had ever suffered from amnesia
   c. they were the best applicants
   d. unknown

3. Sally Ride was a member of the second *Challenger* mission, which was launched into space in _____.
   a. 1977   **b.** 1978   **c.** 1980   **d.** 1983

4. Sally Ride was the _____.
   a. only woman in space
   b. first woman in space
   c. first American woman in space
   d. second woman in space

5. Who thought that Sally Ride's launch into space was an important event for women? _____
   a. the author of the article
   b. Sally Ride
   c. Ride's husband
   d. Ride's father

6. When Ride stated, "As far as I knew, there was nothing else; what you did was launch an arm," she probably meant _____.

   a. she had no desire to be part of the *Challenger* mission

   b. she was totally involved in her work on that project

   c. she was disappointed that she had been assigned to that project

   d. she thought that was all there was to the space program

7. Sally Ride doesn't plan to have children because _____.

   a. she doesn't want any   **c.** her husband doesn't want any

   b. she is too busy with her career   **d.** she is getting too old

8. Who seemed most willing to be interviewed by reporters? _____

   a. Ride's father   **c.** Ride's college roommate

   b. Ride's husband   **d.** Ride's sister

9. Based on this reading, which word *least* describes Sally Ride? _____

   a. adventurous   **b.** private   **c.** resourceful   **d.** tidy

2 More Work with the Apostrophe. Use the example to guide you as you rewrite the following phrases.

   1. the apron of the butcher   the butcher's apron _____

   2. the skyline of Manhattan   _____

   3. the cousins of Tony   _____

   4. the radiator of the Volkswagen _____

   5. the fractured arm of Jack   _____

   6. the cage of the gerbil   _____

   7. the journey of Francis   _____

   8. the servants of Mr. Royal   _____

   9. the orbit of the satellite   _____

  10. the lounge of the clinic   _____

  11. the routine of the veterinarian _____

  12. the halo of the angel   _____

3 Understanding Cartoons. Study the cartoon below, and then answer the questions that follow.

1. What do the reporters seem to be most interested in?

   _____

   _____

2. Which feature of the reporters' faces do you most notice? Why do you think the cartoonist has enlarged this feature?

   _____

   _____

3. What is Ride's reaction to the press? How do you know?

   _____

   _____

4. Whose side does the cartoonist seem to be on in this cartoon? Be sure to offer a reason for your answer.

   _____

   _____

5. Does the cartoonist's picture of the press agree with the description given in the reading passage? Be sure to offer evidence for your answer.

_____

_____

6. Does the cartoonist's picture of Sally Ride agree with the description given in the reading passage? Again, be sure to cite evidence to support your answer.

_____

_____

_____

_____

_____

4 Facts and Opinions. A _fact_ is a statement that can be proven to be true or false. An _opinion_ is a personal thought or attitude about something. Write _fact_ beside each of the following statements that is a fact. Write _opinion_ if the statement is an opinion.

_____ **1.** Most women tend to run around trying to make everyone happy.

_____ **2.** Sally Ride's sister once commented that most women tend to run around trying to make everyone happy.

_____ **3.** Reporters asked Sally Ride many personal questions.

_____ **4.** Reporters should ask anyone in the news as many personal questions as they can so the American public can be informed.

_____ **5.** The president of the United States should only be allowed to serve one four-year term of office.

_____ **6.** In the U.S., presidential elections are held every four years.

_____ **7.** A woman's place is in the home.

_____ **8.** In 1920, women were granted the right to vote.

_____ **9.** Television is a wonderful way to bring the family closer together.

_____ **10.** The average American watches too much television.

5 The Prefix *re-*. The prefix *re-* has two common meanings: *again* (for example, rerun) and *back* (for example, replace). Choose the word from each set that completes the sentence correctly, and write it in the blank.

renew reopen retrieve	**1.** The lawyer was certain that the judge would _____ the case since new evidence had recently come into his possession.
reforming rerunning retracing	**2.** Annabel had spent most of the afternoon _____ the steps of her hectic morning, but her efforts were in vain. She still couldn't find her purse.
recycling reorganization reunion	**3.** His high school class's twenty-fifth _____ was coming soon, but Mr. Beech was having second thoughts about attending, because he had gained quite a few pounds and lost quite a few hairs.
reconstruction recount replacement	**4.** The loser often demands a _____ after a close election if he either suspects foul play or clings to the hope that he might be the winner after all.
recounted rephrased retraced	**5.** William _____ his answer after noting the puzzled expression on the interviewer's face and hoped that his confusing response hadn't ruined his chances of getting the job.
refit refuel repossess	**6.** When Pat learned that the bank was about to _____ her brother-in-law's car, she finally agreed to lend him the money, even though she knew she'd probably never see it again.
reconsider reconstruct refit	**7.** Joe's doctor was able to successfully _____ his shattered leg bone after his terrible automobile accident.
redouble regain retrace	**8.** "Don't worry. If we _____ our efforts, things will work out just fine," the foreman cheerfully advised, in an effort to raise the workers' sagging spirits after they had just experienced a setback.
rebuild reclaim replant	**9.** As part of his evidence to _____ 15,000 acres for the tribe, the lawyer presented a treaty signed by the federal government in 1837 which proved that the land had been granted to the Indians.
reversing revising revoking	**10.** The court slowed Lucy to a walk by _____ her license after she had received three traffic tickets in one month.

6 Compound Words. To complete these sentences correctly, choose a word from **List A** and add a word from **List B** to it. If necessary, use a dictionary to help you complete this exercise.

List A	List B
candle	boat
dare	breakers
guess	bush
handy	coming
heavy	cord
home	devil
look	joyed
motor	light
over	man
rip	out
road	robe
rose	stone
tight	wad
tomb	weight
ward	work
Wind	work

1. Betsy was such a _____ that the airplane pilot prayed she wouldn't wait until the last possible second to pull the _____ of her parachute.

2. Her cousin had always loved gardening so much that after her funeral, Dr. Duke planted a _____ in front of her _____.

3. Mr. Kennedy was such a _____ that he was always on the _____ for inexpensive little items at yard sales that he could use as Christmas and birthday gifts.

4. The boys were glad they had brought their _____ to protect them from the cool breeze when they took their _____ out for a spin on the lake.

5. The trainer warned the _____ boxing champ that if he didn't stop clowning around and start taking his _____ more seriously, he might as well kiss his title good-bye.

6. Wendy went through every item of clothing in her _____ and then burst into tears because she didn't have a single thing to wear to the _____ dance after the football game.

7. When James was unable to repair the kitchen ceiling light, his wife gently reminded him that he had never been much of a _____—to which he spitefully replied, "At least if we eat by _____, I won't have to look at the leftovers you're always serving me."

8. Were you _____ that you immediately knew the answers to this exercise, or were your answers mostly the result of _____?

Words for Study

Samuelson	sextant	liquor	progress
Brooklyn	anchor	routine	instant
voyage	kerosene	glorious	Amazon
compartments	biscuit	canvas	Caribbean
compass	discarded	megaphone	atlas

LESSON 15
New York to France—in a Rowboat

by Tom Mahoney

Strange as it may sound, two men once rowed across the Atlantic Ocean in an open boat—the full 3,250 miles from New York to France. Yet today the Atlantic adventure and the names of its heroes are forgotten.

Frank Samuelson and George Harbo, two men from Norway, lived in Brooklyn and dredged for oysters off New Jersey. In 1896, the year of their daring adventure, Harbo was 30 and Samuelson 26, but both had spent their lives at sea and possessed a strength far greater than their average builds suggested.

"If anybody would row the ocean," Samuelson had told Harbo, "he would make a fortune. People would pay to see the boat." One man couldn't do it, they had agreed, but two men might make the voyage in two months, if they rowed 54 miles a day. So why not try it?

Harbo, a licensed boat pilot, figured out that the best route was eastward by way of the Gulf Stream and the North Atlantic drifts. These currents would add slightly to the speed of a craft going in their direction. Further, this was the heavily traveled North Atlantic shipping route, which promised help in the event of disaster.

For two years, the Norwegians devoted their spare time to completing plans. Finally, they designed a double-pointed, 18-foot craft, with a five-foot beam and eight-inch draft. At both ends were watertight compartments and tanks for drinking water. Into the boat went five pairs of oars, a compass, a sextant, a sea-anchor, an air mattress, signal lights, and five gallons of kerosene for the small stove rigged in the bow. Richard K. Fox, a newspaper publisher, paid for the construction of the boat, and the little white oak craft was named *Fox* in his honor.

Their food included 250 eggs, 100 pounds of sea biscuit, nine pounds of coffee, and plenty of canned meat. All clothing except oilskins and what they were wearing was discarded. No tobacco, liquor, or sails were taken aboard.

A crowd of 2,000 gathered the afternoon of June 6, 1896, to see them off. The weather was perfect, but there was an air of gloom. "This is suicide," was a common comment.

"We'll see you all in France or in heaven!" shouted Harbo cheerfully as the *Fox* pushed off. Harbor whistles saluted the boat as it skimmed down the bay with both Harbo and Samuelson rowing. When the *Fox* passed out to sea, the two Norwegians began their routine, which called for 15½ hours of rowing a day for each man. At first, the weather was glorious; but trouble began with the oil stove. It was hard to keep lighted even in a mild breeze. They had little coffee and soon had to eat their eggs raw.

On the fourth night out, Harbo was asleep under the canvas shelter. Suddenly, he sat up and cried: "Something bumped us!"

As they listened, it came again, a bump and a scrape across the bottom. Then, something white flashed in the dark water alongside.

"A shark!" said Harbo.

For two days the shark swam with the boat while the oarsmen, undisturbed, continued their rowing.

A week out, the adventurers met a schooner bound from Canada to New York.

"Come alongside and we'll take you aboard!" the captain shouted through his megaphone.

"No thanks," Samuelson shouted back. "We're on a voyage."

"Where are you bound?"

"Europe."

With her crew shaking their heads, the Canadian ship sailed on.

The next day, Sunday, the oarsmen experienced their first bad weather. A heavy gale blew up from the east, almost dead ahead. Waves rose higher and higher until they washed over the *Fox*. At 9 a.m. the two men gave up rowing and tossed out the sea anchor. By 5 p.m., Harbo figured that their progress for the day had been 25 miles backward!

Ten days later, a German ship came into sight. Harbo hoisted an American flag, and the steamer responded with her colors.

"Are you shipwrecked?" the steamer's skipper shouted.

"No. Bound for Europe."

"Are you crazy?"

"No, indeed." On the Norwegians rowed, sometimes singing, but usually pulling their oars in silence.

On July 7 a westerly gale blew up, and for two days the exhausted oarsmen battled huge waves. It was a grim fight. Ten times a day the tiny craft had to be bailed out. Then, on the second night, a giant wave bore down on them.

"Look out!" shouted Samuelson.

"We'll never clear it!" gasped Harbo.

In an instant the *Fox* was overturned and the two men were struggling in icy water. But even for this emergency they had made plans. Each wore a life belt, fastened to the boat by rope.

Also, the keel had been provided with a rail to which the voyagers could cling.

After several attempts, they righted the boat, crawled aboard and began desperately to bail. Some of their food had been swept away; their clothes were soaked. Sleepless and hungry, they presented a sorry sight as the sun rose over a quieter sea. They stripped and wrung out their soaked clothing. Then they resumed rowing to take the stiffness from their swollen joints.

But there were other problems. Wind, sun, and salt water had turned the backs of their hands into raw flesh. An even graver problem was their low food supply. While previously it had been amusing to joke with passing vessels, it was now a matter of life or death to hail one.

Help appeared on July 15 in the shape of a vessel bound for Canada. The oarsmen tied a blanket to an oar and began to wave it. At last, the ship turned toward the starving oarsmen. The vessel turned out to be from their birthplace in Norway. After a joyful reunion with seamen like themselves, the two adventurers filled the *Fox*'s water tanks, stocked her with fresh food, and continued their voyage.

With half their voyage behind them, the weather continued fair and for more than a week they averaged 65 miles a day. On August 1 they sighted land—the southwestern tip of England. On August 7 their voyage ended when Samuelson and Harbo stepped ashore in France to the cheers of thousands.

Did the men make the fortune they had dreamed of? No. The problem was that the rowboat that had crossed the Atlantic looked just like any other rowboat, and people would not pay to see it. Greatly disappointed, both men disappeared from the public spotlight and finally went back to Norway. In 1946, Samuelson died in an old people's home. The Norwegian newspapers were kinder to him in death than they had been in life. "The world will not soon see his like again," wrote one reporter.

1 About the Reading. State whether the following quotes from the reading passage are statements of fact or statements of opinion. Then explain the reason for your answer in good sentence form. Be sure to use information from the reading to support your answer.

1. "We'll see you all in France or in heaven!"

_____

_____

2. "Something bumped us!"

_____

_____

3. "We'll never clear it."

_____

_____

4. "This is suicide."

_____

_____

5. "If anybody would row the ocean, he would make a fortune."

_____

_____

6. "The world will not soon see his like again."

_____

_____

2 What Do You Think? Describe a situation in which you might be willing to risk your life for a fortune. Remember that fortune does not always refer to money. Fortune can refer to success in general.

_____

_____

_____

_____

3 Synonyms. Match each word with its synonym.

| agreement | conflict | decrease | furthermore | illegal | occupation |
| bulletin | consideration | faraway | glorious | nerveless | suspect |

_____ **1.** announcement   _____ **7.** reduce

_____ **2.** banned   _____ **8.** remote

_____ **3.** distrust   _____ **9.** splendid

_____ **4.** livelihood   _____ **10.** struggle

_____ **5.** moreover   _____ **11.** thoughtfulness

_____ **6.** pact   _____ **12.** unafraid

4 Antonyms. Match each word with its antonym.

| abbreviate | defense | heavenly | irresponsible | reckless | retrieve |
| ashore | disperse | inexperienced | manmade | remote | watertight |

_____ **1.** aboard   _____ **7.** lengthen

_____ **2.** cautious   _____ **8.** natural

_____ **3.** dependable   _____ **9.** nearby

_____ **4.** discard   _____ **10.** offense

_____ **5.** gather   _____ **11.** veteran

_____ **6.** leaky   _____ **12.** worldly

5 The Prefix *pre-*. The prefix *pre-* means *before or happening earlier in time*. Use the words listed below to complete the following sentences correctly.

precooked	preheat	prejudged	prepay	preshrunk	preview
predated	prehistory	premedical	preschool	pretest	prewar

1. "I'm sorry I was so harsh with you. I guess I _____ you as a lousy actress, but your work tonight proved I was dead wrong," the producer said sheepishly after Jill's faultless performance on opening night.

2. Anthony hoped that although he had forgotten to _____ the oven, it wouldn't affect the new recipe he was preparing for his guests that evening.

3. At 3:30 the _____ children left the zoo and were pleasantly surprised when the adults treated them to ice cream sodas before dropping them off at their homes.

4. Franklin thought that if he _____ the rent check, his landlord might believe that the only reason his payment was late was that he had forgotten to mail it.

5. "If this movie is anything like the _____," remarked Pearl, "it's going to win the prize for most boring picture of the year."

6. Months before the first shot was fired, the _____ movement of troops made the people of Europe tense and uneasy.

7. On the first day, the students took a _____ so the instructor would have a fairly good idea of how much they already knew about auto repair.

8. Until reading that her new pantsuit had been _____, Miss Adams was uncertain about whether she could wash it.

9. Figuring out how to earn enough money for _____ school was the next step, once Herb decided he wanted to be a psychiatrist.

10. _____ is the study of mankind in the period before written or recorded history.

11. Simply having to heat up the _____ ham made preparing dinner take only a few minutes.

12. Learning that he had to _____ for the tools he wanted to send for, Mr. Cooper replied, "Forget it. I don't fork over my hard-earned money for anything until I see it."

6 Bodies of Water. Use a dictionary, encyclopedia, or atlas to answer the following questions. To save yourself some time and effort, skim all the questions before you begin.

1. Match each word with its definition.

| lake | ocean | river | sea |

_____ **A.** a large body of salt water that is completely or partly surrounded by land or is a tract of water within an ocean

_____ **B.** a large inland body of fresh or salt water

_____ **C.** a large natural stream of water emptying into an ocean, lake, or other body of water

_____ **D.** the entire body of salt water that covers about 72 percent of the earth's surface

2. Place the bodies of water listed below in their proper categories. Use each name only once.

Amazon	Dead	Louise	North
Arctic	Great Salt	Michigan	Pacific
Atlantic	Huron	Mississippi	Snake
Caribbean	Indian	Nile	South China

Lakes	Oceans	Rivers	Seas

3. Use the bodies of water in Question 2 to answer these questions.

a. What is the world's longest river? _____

b. What is the earth's largest body of water? _____

c. Which sea is located north of South America? _____

d. Which lake is located in the state of Utah? _____

e. Which lake is located entirely in the country of Canada? _____

1 Word Review. Use the words listed below to fill in the blanks correctly.

Amazon	compass	morphine	oilskin	satellite
Broadway	generation	myth	poverty	sextant
capsule	megaphone	Nile	reins	shuttle

_____ 1. a compartment of an aircraft or spacecraft designed to accommodate a crew; a covering for a dose of medicine

_____ 2. a compound extracted from opium; repeated doses cause addiction

_____ 3. a device used to figure geographical direction; also, a V-shaped device used for drawing circles

_____ 4. a funnel-shaped device used to direct and make one's voice louder

_____ 5. a river in eastern Africa

_____ 6. a river of South America that flows north and then east to the Atlantic Ocean

_____ 7. a small body orbiting a planet

_____ 8. a story dealing with gods, goddesses, ancestors, and heroes

_____ 9. a train, bus, or plane making short trips between two points; a device used in weaving to carry a thread back and forth between other threads

_____ 10. an instrument used by seamen to measure the height of heavenly bodies

_____ 11. cloth treated with oil so that it is waterproof

_____ 12. long, narrow leather straps used by a rider or driver to control a horse or other animal

_____ 13. the average length of time between the birth of parents and the birth of their offspring

_____ 14. the main theater district of New York City

_____ 15. the state or condition of being poor

2 Word Review. Write the letter of the best answer on the line.

1. A patient who has amnesia suffers from _____.
   a. acid indigestion   **b.** eyestrain   **c.** high blood pressure   **d.** memory loss

2. What was the capital of the former Soviet Union? _____
   a. London   **b.** Moscow   **c.** Paris   **d.** Warsaw

3. Which word describes a person who is able to make the most out of what is available? _____
   a. accommodating   **b.** fearless   **c.** independent   **d.** resourceful

4. If you wanted to learn more about the god Apollo, in which section of the library would you look? _____
   a. geography   **b.** history   **c.** mythology   **d.** travel

5. Which word describes your chances of winning the lottery? _____
   a. endless   **b.** plentiful   **c.** remote   **d.** unlimited

6. Which word describes your likely reaction if you learned you had indeed just won the lottery? _____
   a. irresponsible   **b.** stunned   **c.** sober   **d.** ungrateful

7. For which of the following do you have to knead dough? _____
   a. cupcakes   **b.** doughnuts   **c.** corn bread   **d.** pancakes

8. A snobbish person usually lacks _____.
   a. compassion   **b.** opinions   **c.** envy   **d.** self-interest

9. Which country would you visit if you wanted to see the Nile River? _____
   a. Egypt   **b.** Japan   **c.** Norway   **d.** Russia

10. Which word means to store away in a neat and compact way? _____
    a. reconstruct   **b.** refit   **c.** stint   **d.** stow

11. Which government agency is not concerned with investigating criminal activities? _____
    a. CIA   **b.** FBI   **c.** IRS   **d.** NASA

12. A synonym for behold is _____.
    a. gaze   **b.** glance   **c.** glare   **d.** grasp

13. If you assume something is true, you _____.
    a. doubt that it is true   **c.** hope that it is true
    b. have confirmed that it is true   **d.** take for granted that it is true

14. Which of the following is often considered a symbol of good fortune? _____.

    a. a cat's paw   **b.** a coonskin cap   **c.** a peacock's feather   **d.** a rabbit's foot

15. Which symbol is often used in a cartoon when one of the characters has an inspiration? _____.

    a. a giant   **b.** a lightbulb   **c.** a question mark   **d.** an anchor

3 How Would You Classify It? Match the words in the list below with their proper categories. Use each word only once.

astronaut	*Challenger*	cosmonaut	encyclopedia	moon	rifle	sextant
barrel	cinnamon	Cupid	kerosene	motorcycle	scarlet	whale

_____   **1.** NASA employee

_____   **2.** color

_____   **3.** container

_____   **4.** firearm

_____   **5.** fuel

_____   **6.** god

_____   **7.** instrument

_____   **8.** mammal

_____   **9.** reference book

_____   **10.** Russian space program employee

_____   **11.** satellite

_____   **12.** spacecraft

_____   **13.** spice

_____   **14.** vehicle

4 Facts and Opinions. Write four examples of statements of fact and four examples of statements of opinion. Study the examples before you begin.

Facts

Example: In 1867, the United States purchased Alaska for $ 7.2 million.

1. _____

_____

2. _____

_____

3. _____

_____

4. _____

_____

Opinions

Example: The least pleasant season of the year in the Northeast is winter.

1. _____

_____

2. _____

_____

3. _____

_____

4. _____

_____

5 Review of the Apostrophe and Capitalization. In the sentences below, 29 words need to be capitalized. Also, three words in each sentence need apostrophes. Rewrite each sentence below, making the necessary changes.

1. ever since shed read the story of cupid in her brothers greek mythology book, kate wished that such a god really did exist who would shoot an arrow of passion into dr. springs heart.

_____

_____

_____

_____

2. "id meet you at grand central station, but manhattans traffic is so bad youd be better off just taking a taxi to west end avenue," adam told aunt mary, who was coming to visit for the weekend.

_____

_____

_____

_____

3. "theyll never have time to visit grants tomb if theyre planning to spend the afternoon in central park," said tom who quickly added, "but then, who wants to see a tomb on such a glorious autumn afternoon."

_____

_____

_____

_____

4. after reading the article about sally rides life in an old issue of time magazine at the dentists office, tony was certain that her work on the challenger had been much more relaxing than all the interviews shed had to suffer through.

_____

_____

_____

_____

6 Five-Letter Words.

- The letters of the word in each box can be used to form another word. Use the clues to help you figure out what that other word is.
- Then put the number of the clue into the circle. The circled numbers in each row and column will add up to 34.
- After you have figured out a word, write its first letter in the correct blank at the bottom of the page. When all the blanks are filled in, you will have spelled the name of the world's largest inland sea.
- To help you, the first and last clues have been filled in.

MOORS ◯ _____	TUN AS ◯ _____	AMONG ① MANGO	DREAD ⑯ ADDER	= 34
BELOW ◯ _____	FLIER ◯ _____	LEASE ◯ _____	KNEAD ◯ _____	= 34
HEART ◯ _____	KNITS ◯ _____	RELAY ◯ _____	LIVED ◯ _____	= 34
THORN ◯ _____	ASIDE ◯ _____	RANGE ◯ _____	BLEAT ◯ _____	= 34
= 34	= 34	= 34	= 34	

Clues

✓1. A fruit that rhymes with tango
2. The joint between the forearm and upper arm
3. In paintings and cartoons, he is often pictured with horns, a tail, and carrying a pitchfork.
4. Thoughts or opinions
5. Like people, this piece of furniture has legs
6. An antonym for late
7. A firearm designed to be fired from the shoulder

8. Kitchens and dens are examples of _____.
9. The sisters of your mother and father
10. Nude or unclothed
11. The third planet from the sun
12. A feeling of rage
13. The opposite of south
14. To give off a strong, foul smell
15. A stand for an artist to put his canvases on
✓16. A kind of snake

The world's largest inland sea:

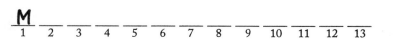

M __ __ __ __ __ __ __ __ __ __ __ __   __ __ A
1 2 3 4 5 6 7 8 9 10 11 12 13   14 15 16

Food

Some people eat to live; other people live to eat. In this last unit of Book 6, we present food in all its glory: from its early American roots to some landmark improvements and current trends. Plus we'll see just what can happen when our bodies revolt against what we put into them.

The reading for Lesson 16, "As American as Apple Pie," describes the importance of the apple in colonial America and tells how Johnny Appleseed came to be a famous American folk hero.

The reading for Lesson 17, "Digestive Disturbances," offers an overview of the symptoms, causes, and treatments of some common digestive ailments. It also suggests ways to keep your digestive system running smoothly.

What is mealtime like for an American family? The selection for Lesson 18 shows how one family acts as its members gather for their morning meal. This reading, "A Breakfast Scene," is taken from a famous play entitled *A Raisin in the Sun*.

What do Americans eat? In Lesson 19, we take an interesting and informative walk through the history of "American Food." We'll see what Americans were eating in the days before Columbus landed in the New World right up to the foods we enjoy today.

Finally, in Lesson 20, "The Wizard of Alabama" describes the life of George Washington Carver—an American scientist whose experiments with plants did much to improve both the diet and general quality of many people's lives.

Words for Study

orchards	transformed	puddings	endure
colonists	vinegar	agriculture	warrior
plague	methods	adapted	sear
survivors	preserving	insecticides	villages
reasonable	fritters	frontier	portrayed

LESSON 16
As American as Apple Pie
by Peter Wynne

Apples have always been important in America, especially in the North. In fact, planting apple orchards was among the first tasks the settlers in the early colonies undertook. Crab apple trees were already growing wild in the woods of North America when the settlers arrived, but they made no effort to put these trees in orchards. Instead, like Johnny Appleseed, they grew their trees from seeds. Only they used seeds imported from Europe.

Apples were important for many reasons. Very high on the list was as a source of cider. The colonists needed something to drink, but they did not consider the pure drinking water in America because they were in the habit of avoiding the water in Europe—for good reason. For the most part, water in Europe was so impure that it wasn't worth one's life to drink it. In England, for example, it was the standard practice when someone died of plague for his survivors to throw his bedding into the nearest lake or river. So the only choices the American colonists considered as reasonable drinks were ones they were used to—beer and wine of some sort or another. Hard cider is actually classified as a wine.

In addition to drinking cider, the colonists used it as the raw material for other important products. For one thing, cider was easily transformed into cider vinegar. The vinegar was used in pickling, one of the important methods of preserving vegetables and fruits for winter before the coming of canned goods.

Apple cider also could be used to make a type of brandy popularly called applejack. When strong enough, the applejack could be used to preserve fruits such as peaches, plums, and cherries. Beyond that, strong

spirits, including apple spirits, found plenty of use in early medicine.

Beyond cider and its by-products, apples were used as food for livestock which were allowed to graze in early orchards and, of course, as food for the colonists themselves. The expression "as American as apple pie" wasn't the product of a poet's imagination. Apple dishes of one kind or another could be found at just about every colonist's meal, especially in New England. The apple was made into pies and fritters and puddings—a host of dishes.

One quality that made apples especially popular in the early American kitchen was that they lasted. If handled gently and stored with care in October, they might keep until the following March. Apples that would not keep in storage could be dried or made into apple butter.

Often apples for drying were peeled, and the peels and cores were dried separately for later use in brewing a kind of beer.

In colonial America, apples were popular not just because of their wide variety of uses. The apple trees did not require a lot of attention. Insects apparently did not attack the trees or the apples to the extent they do today. When reading old records of American agriculture, one seldom finds references to insect damage. The plants and fruits that the colonists introduced to this country were foreign to the diets of the native insects. As long as their native foods were available in the forests, these insects stayed pretty much in the wilderness.

But when the forests were replaced by farms, native insects adapted themselves to the new conditions. In addition, insect pests from Europe were introduced into America, concealed among the plants and seeds that the colonists and later generations brought with them. It sometimes took years for the foreign insects to adapt fully, but they did.

Insecticides were introduced during the 1800s to combat the insect pests that did exist. Despite this fact, the insect problem seems to have worsened. In 1944, a work written by one of America's top experts on fruit growing indicated that more than twenty insects were causing trouble for apple growers. Today, bulletins issued by the United States Department of Agriculture list more than thirty insects that feed on apples.

Why does the insect problem seem to be getting worse? Apples today are bigger and sweeter than their earlier cousins. These qualities may make them a more desirable food to a greater number of insect pests. Too, apples today are mostly grown in huge orchards. These orchards add up to big hunks of bug bait. Once America's insects learned to include apples in their diets, they became a problem and this state of affairs has remained ever since.

* * *

In addition to being a source of food for centuries, the apple has also been a source of folklore. One of the most popular American myths is about Johnny Appleseed. The folk tales about Johnny Appleseed are based on a man named John Chapman who lived on the Ohio-Indiana frontier. He was a strange but pleasant fellow who enjoyed his liquor and loved plants and animals. He spent his time planting apple seeds, which he obtained from cider mills.

One of the people who helped to create the myth of Johnny Appleseed was a woman named Rosella Rice who knew Chapman when she was a youngster living in Ohio. When she grew up she wrote about him. But instead of writing about him exactly as she remembered him, she used her imagination to transform him from an odd and colorful fellow into an American saint—Johnny Appleseed. The information about Johnny Appleseed which follows is taken from her stories.

She describes Johnny as having long hair and a long beard and dressing oddly in old clothes which he received in exchange for his work—planting apple seeds. Sometimes he carried a bag or two of seeds on an old horse. But more often he bore them on his back, going from place to place on the wild frontier, clearing a little patch, surrounding it with a crudely made fence and planting seeds therein. He had little orchards all through Pennsylvania, Ohio, and Indiana.

According to Rice, Johnny was never known to hunt any animal or to give any animal pain. One time, when overtaken by night while traveling, he crawled into a hollow log and slept till morning. In the other end of the log were a bear and her cubs. Johnny said he knew the bear would not hurt him, and that there was room enough for all.

The Indians liked Johnny and treated him very kindly. They regarded him as a man above his fellows. He could endure pain like an Indian warrior; he could thrust pins into his flesh without a shiver. Indeed, he could endure pain so well that his way of treating a wound or sore was to sear it with a hot iron and then treat it as a burn.

In 1838. according to legend, Johnny, who was then well on in years, decided to head further west to escape the villages that were springing up. Stagecoaches loaded with travelers were common; schools were being built; and brick houses were taking the place of lowly cabins.

During the next few years, he returned to Indiana several times. The last time was in the year he died, 1845. One day in the spring of that year, he visited a friend in western Indiana. The friend, as usual, greeted him warmly. That evening, Johnny refused to eat anything except some bread and milk which he had while sitting on the doorstep and looking out on the setting sun. The next morning, when a physician came to the house to examine Johnny, he saw that Johnny, near death, was perfectly calm and peaceful. His life had been filled with unselfishness. His memory would live on, and his deeds would live anew every spring in the apple blossoms he loved so well.

1 About the Reading. Put the letter of the correct answer on the line.

1. In the American colonies, the major use of apples was for _____.
   a. brandy   **b.** cider   **c.** fritters   **d.** puddings

2. Cider vinegar was important to the colonists because _____.
   a. it could be used to make brandy
   b. it enabled them to preserve fruits and vegetables
   c. it was something to drink when cider was not available
   d. it was the major source of medicine

3. A main reason that the apple was especially popular in early American cooking was that _____.

   a. an apple a day keeps the doctor away

   b. apple orchards were common in New England

   c. it could be stored for a long period of time

   d. it tasted good in many different types of dishes

4. As farms and villages replaced the forests, one of the effects mentioned by the author was _____.

   a. farmers were confronted with an increasingly difficult insect problem

   b. consumers began to prefer canned goods to preserved fruits and vegetables

   c. folk tales such as Johnny Appleseed became popular because people wished to remember "the good old days"

   d. people no longer drank so much cider because drinking water became increasingly pure

5. Which of the following is *not* cited as a possible cause of the increasing problem apple growers are experiencing with insects?_____.

   a. Apples today are larger than apples of years ago.

   b. Apples today are sweeter than apples of years ago.

   c. Because apple trees are grown in orchards rather than scattered about the countryside, insects find it easy to attack the trees.

   d. Foreign insects do not have trouble adapting to American varieties of apples.

6. The folk tales about Johnny Appleseed are based on the life of _____.

   a. John Chapman   b. Peter Wynne   c. Rosella Rice   d. E. P. Dutton

7. The folk tales about Johnny Appleseed tell of his _____.

   a. hunting and fishing trips

   b. trying to make a name for himself

   c. planting apple orchards throughout Ohio, Pennsylvania, and Indiana

   d. friendship with Rosella Rice

8. According to the folk tales, the Indians admired Johnny Appleseed for his _____.

   a. compassion   b. courage   c. honesty   d. resourcefulness

9. Based on the information in this reading passage, which of the following does *not* describe Johnny Appleseed as portrayed in Rosella Rice's tales?_____.

   a. a drinking man   b. a lover of nature   c. a man of daring   d. a wanderer

10. According to Rosella Rice, Johnny thought his memory would live on because _____.

   a. his children would continue to tell stories about him

   b. he believed that his diary would someday be published

   c. he knew Rosella Rice's stories about him would continue to be popular

   d. the apple trees he planted would continue to grow and remind people of him

2 A Recipe for Apple Fritters. Read the recipe for apple fritters, and then answer the questions that follow.

Aplyn Fruturs

For to mak Fruturs: Nym flowre and eyryn and grynd peper and mak therto a batour and par aplyn and kyt hem to brode penys and cast hem theryn and fry hem in batour wyth fresch grees and serve it forthe.

Did you have any trouble reading this recipe? Believe it or not, this is English—English as it was spoken and written from about 1125 to about 1475.

1. List five words from the recipe that are the same now as they were during the 1125–1475 period of history.

_____   _____   _____   _____   _____

2. Study the recipe and then match the words with their modern spellings.

batter	cut	grease	take
broad	eggs	pare	them

_____ **A.** nym   _____ **E.** kyt

_____ **B.** eyryn   _____ **F.** hem

_____ **C.** batour   _____ **G.** brode

_____ **D.** par   _____ **H.** grees

3. Study the recipe and then write the modern English spellings for these words.

A. fruturs _____   **D.** mak _____

B. flowre _____   **E.** penys _____

C. peper _____   **F.** fresch _____

4. Most modern recipes give measurements. For example, a modern recipe might tell you to use 1 cup flour. Why do you think measurements were not used in very old recipes?

_____

_____

5. Do you think the English we speak and write will be as strange to English-speaking people living five hundred years from now as the English in the recipe is to us? Give reasons to support your opinion.

_____

_____

3 Words with More Than One Meaning. Each of the underlined words in the sentences below has more than one meaning. Check the meaning that applies to the word as it has been used in the sentence.

1. "The apple was made into pies and fritters and puddings—a <u>host</u> of dishes."

_____ an army

_____ a living thing that harbors and provides food for another living thing

_____ a great number

_____ one who entertains guests

2. After three-year-old Linda had been examined in the emergency room, she was moved to the children's <u>ward</u>.

_____ a large room in a hospital usually holding six or more patients

_____ a section of a city or a town

_____ a section of a hospital for the care of a particular group of patients

_____ any person under the protection or care of another

3. The governor's <u>staff</u> worked round the clock to have the budget review prepared in time for the upcoming television debate.

_____ a group of assistants or workers

_____ a pole upon which a flag is displayed

_____ a stick, rod, or cane carried as an aid in walking

_____ in music, a set of lines and their spaces upon which notes are written or printed

4. When the union boss <u>polled</u> the workers, he was surprised to learn that their main complaints had nothing at all to do with money.

_____ to cast a vote or ballot

_____ to question a sample group of people in order to survey public opinion

_____ to trim or cut off hair, wool, or horns

5. The Quincys decided to purchase the Southern mansion despite the retired caretaker's warnings that <u>spirits</u> had walked its marbled floors since as far back as the Civil War.

_____ ghosts

_____ liquor

_____ one's mood or emotional state

6. As Doc Parker dabbed ointment on the sobbing gunfighter's forehead, he said, "Don't carry on so, Matt. You know as well as I do that the bullet only grazed you."

_____ to feed on growing grasses

_____ to put livestock out to feed

_____ to touch lightly in passing; to skim or brush

7. An annoyed English gentleman once asked, "What business have people to get children to plague their neighbors?"

_____ a disease which is usually deadly

_____ a sudden occurrence which usually causes destruction

_____ to annoy or upset

8. Of Helen, a figure in Greek mythology whose beauty caused men to start a war, an English poet wrote, "Was this the face that launched a thousand ships?"

_____ any large, open motorboat

_____ to put into action

_____ to hurl or throw

9. James Whistler felt honored when, in 1891, the Society of British Artists purchased a canvas he had titled *The Artist's Mother*.

_____ a heavy material used for making tents and sails

_____ a piece of such a material on which a painting is made, especially an oil painting

_____ the floor of a ring in which boxing or wrestling takes place

10. An English writer once said, "Wrong opinions and practices slowly yield to fact and argument."

_____ to give way to what is stronger or better

_____ to furnish or give a return

_____ the profit obtained from an investment

4 Wake Up and Smell the Coffee! If you're worth your salt, you can match these food idioms to their meanings. Use your noodle to fill in the blanks. Are idioms your cup of tea?

a piece of cake	cost peanuts	in a pickle
a tough nut to crack	couch potato	nest egg
apples and oranges	cream of the crop	nutty as a fruitcake
as easy as pie	cry over spilt milk	pie in the sky
big cheese	don't upset the apple cart	rotten egg
brownie points	egg on	smart cookie
butterfingers	forbidden fruit	the apple of one's eye
butter up	from soup to nuts	to have egg on one's face
carrot top	go bananas	two peas in a pod
cool as a cucumber	in a nutshell	walk on eggshells

_____ **1.** two things so different they cannot be compared

_____ **2.** an evil person

_____ **3.** briefly

_____ **4.** credit for doing good deeds

_____ **5.** in trouble

_____ **6.** redhead

_____ **7.** a very intelligent person

_____ **8.** cost very little

_____ **9.** someone who lies around watching TV a lot

_____ **10.** the best

_____ **11.** someone who is difficult to deal with

_____ **12.** very simple

_____ **13.** a clumsy person

_____ **14.** very calm

_____ **15.** to encourage someone to do something

_____ **16.** two people who look alike or who are always together

_____ **17.** something desirable that is bad for you

_____ **18.** from the beginning to the end

_____ **19.** go crazy

_____ **20.** to be sad over something that's in the past

_____ 21. an important person

_____ 22. to praise and flatter someone to get what you want

_____ 23. savings for the future

_____ 24. crazy

_____ 25. a reward that you'll probably never get

_____ 26. very easy

_____ 27. one's favorite person

_____ 28. to feel embarrassed or foolish

_____ 29. don't cause trouble

_____ 30. to be careful not to upset someone

5 Using the Apostrophe with Plural Words. _Plural_, if you remember, means _more than one_. For example, one apple, two apples. _Apples_ is the plural form of apple. When the plural form of a word ends in _s_, add just the apostrophe to show ownership. Study the two examples carefully, and then write the plural form of ownership for the following.

1. the growth of the colonies   _the colonies' growth_

2. the defense of the players   _the players' defense_

3. the pranks of the rascals   _____

4. the construction of the skyscrapers _____

5. the ripeness of the bananas   _____

6. the dismissal of the cartoonists   _____

7. the friendliness of the Canadians   _____

8. the red glare of the rockets   _____

9. the entertainment of the visitors   _____

10. the boldness of the daredevils   _____

11. the roar of the motors   _____

12. the availability of the nurses   _____

6 The Suffix -tion. Use the words below to complete this exercise correctly.

accommodations	compositions	explanations	infections	reservation
addiction	definitions	extractions	inflation	starvation
combination	exhaustion	graduation	investigations	temptation

_____ **1.** what a hotel offers

_____ **2.** what a traveler makes to get an airline ticket

_____ **3.** what being without food can cause

_____ **4.** what commissions and detectives conduct

_____ **5.** what consumers always complain about

_____ **6.** what dentists perform

_____ **7.** what the dictionary contains

_____ **8.** what drug abuse can lead to

_____ **9.** what English students write

_____ **10.** what insect bites can cause

_____ **11.** what overwork can lead to

_____ **12.** what parents often demand when their children come home late

_____ **13.** what sinners are warned not to give in to

_____ **14.** what students look forward to

_____ **15.** what you might need to know to open a locker or safe

Words for Study

heartburn	acid reflux	infection	pus
diarrhea	antacid	feces	abdomen
constipation	surgery	fiber	fatal
salivary	frequent	antibiotics	diverticulitis
enzymes	bowel	refined	gallbladder
excreted	virus	appendicitis	crystal

LESSON 17
Digestive Disturbances

Heartburn. Diarrhea. Constipation. All are common problems of the digestive system—problems that most people have had at one time or another. What causes these embarrassing, unpleasant, and sometimes painful conditions? We'll explore the symptoms, causes, and treatments for each one. But first, let's take a look at the process of digestion.

The human digestive system changes the food that we eat into energy for our bodies to use. Just thinking about, seeing, or smelling food gets the process of digestion started by stimulating the salivary glands. When we chew, our teeth break up the food into small bits. Saliva turns the chewed food into a soft mass that's easy to swallow.

Once it is swallowed, food heads down the esophagus to the stomach. In the stomach, digestive juices and enzymes help to further break down the food into a thick liquid or paste. Then the thick liquid is squeezed, little by little, into the small intestines. As the food moves through the small intestines, nutrients are taken in and sent to the bloodstream. Anything that cannot be used to feed the cells passes into the large intestines and is eventually excreted.

Common Digestive Conditions

HEARTBURN   Heartburn is a burning feeling in the chest that can travel to the neck, throat, and even face. It is caused by stomach acid flowing back up through the esophagus from the stomach. The acid irritates the esophagus. More than one out of three people in the U.S. suffers from chronic heartburn or acid reflux.

Many different factors can cause heartburn. Cigarettes, alcohol, and rich or spicy foods may all be triggers. Heartburn can even happen after a

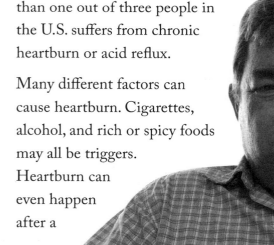

person eats a very large meal. One way to prevent heartburn is to avoid whatever causes the problem. Mild cases can be treated with over-the-counter antacids. More severe cases of acid reflux may require prescription drugs or even surgery.

DIARRHEA   Diarrhea is having frequent runny or watery bowel movements. In the U.S., it is most often brought on by a virus or infection. A common cause of diarrhea is a virus commonly called the "stomach flu." Many different viruses can cause the stomach flu, which can travel quickly through an office, day-care center, or school. The symptoms may last only a day or two.

But it is important for those suffering with it to drink plenty of liquids so that their bodies do not lose too much water.

Infections that cause diarrhea can be easily spread to others. They can be spread through dirty hands, food or water, through some pets, or by direct contact with feces (such as through dirty diapers or the toilet). To help prevent diarrhea, be sure to wash your hands regularly. Keep bathroom surfaces clean. Wash fruits and vegetables before eating. Keep uncooked meats in the refrigerator and cook fully. By taking these steps you can lower your chances of getting or spreading diarrhea.

CONSTIPATION   Constipation occurs when a person has infrequent or difficult bowel movements. It may also cause stools that are hard, dry, or unusually large. Most of the time, constipation is caused by a diet that doesn't include enough water and fiber. Both help the bowel move properly.

People who eat diets rich in fats and processed sugars may find that they're constipated more often.

Sometimes, medicine can cause constipation. Stress can also lead to constipation. Constipation isn't usually a big cause for concern. It can often be fixed with healthy eating and exercise habits.

Common Causes of Digestive Problems

STRESS   Stress of all kinds—be it emotional, mental, or physical—can take its toll on the digestive system. Mental and emotional stressors include things like anger, worry, and fear. Physical stressors can include infections and surgery. All of these can have major effects on our digestive systems. Even harmful substances in the environment can cause stress on our bodies. When we feel stress, our bodies send energy, blood, and oxygen from the digestive organs to other areas of the body. This is a natural reaction to stress, but it robs our digestive organs of what they need to work properly.

ANTIBIOTICS   Antibiotics are necessary to fight infections in our bodies. But taking them can kill many of the healthy bacteria in our digestive tracts. Antibiotics also affect the number of bad bacteria found in the gut that the healthy bacteria are there to protect us from. Once antibiotics are stopped, there is a chance for things such as yeasts to move in. These things can cause damage to the gut wall. And they can create poisons that can affect the immune system.

POOR DIET   Eating a diet low in fiber and high in fat and processed foods is a recipe for digestive disaster. The digestive system needs fiber to help speed food through the digestive tract.

A lack of fiber means a greater risk of the body taking some of the harmful substances from food waste into the bloodstream. Refined carbohydrates are made from sugar and flour stripped of dozens of nutrients in the refining process. The body needs these nutrients to help digest foods properly. When refined carbohydrates are not fully digested, they can turn into simple sugars and alcohols. Yeast and bacteria can feed on sugar or alcohol, causing indigestion, gas, and bloating.

DRUGS   Many people rely on medicines to get and stay healthy. Medicines are necessary to cure diseases. But all drugs and chemicals are basically harmful to the digestive system. Some common medications can irritate the lining of the stomach. This can cause trouble with digestion.

GENES   Our genes play an important role in how well our digestive systems work. Problems that family members have are often passed down to other members. It is especially important to work toward maintaining digestive health if a certain condition runs in your family.

Keeping Your Digestive System Healthy

A healthy lifestyle should keep your digestive system running smoothly. That means doing things like:

- eating healthy foods
- exercising regularly
- controlling your weight
- not smoking
- drinking little or no alcohol
- reducing stress

All of these things should help keep your digestive system in top form.

1 According to the Author. The article tells about three digestive conditions and describes symptoms, causes, and treatments for each. Write at least one symptom, one cause, and one treatment for each of the conditions below.

a. Heartburn

symptom: _____

cause: _____

treatment: _____

b. Diarrhea

symptom: _____

cause: _____

treatment: _____

c. Constipation

symptom: _____

cause: _____

treatment: _____

2 About the Reading. Each statement below is missing a key piece of information. Review the part of the reading called "Common Causes of Digestive Problems," and then rewrite each statement correctly. Read the example before you begin.

1. Physical stress can have a negative impact on the digestive system.

   All kinds of stress—emotional, mental, and physical—can have a negative impact on the digestive system.

2. Antibiotics harm our bodies by killing off healthy bacteria.

   _____

   _____

3. Eating foods that contain refined carbohydrates can be disastrous for your digestive tract.

   _____

   _____

4. Medicines are good for us because they help us stay healthy.

   _____

   _____

3 Using the Apostrophe with Plural Words. Write the plural form of possession for the following. Review the examples in Lesson 16 before you begin.

1. the recipes of the chefs _____

2. the output of the steel mills _____

3. the thoughtlessness of the litterbugs _____

4. the settlement of the strikers _____

5. the toys of the kittens _____

6. the distrust of the villagers _____

7. the possessions of the roommates _____

8. the beauty of the mountains _____

9. the findings of the researchers _____

10. the affection of the sweethearts _____

4 The Suffix -*sion*. Use the words listed below to complete the sentences.

admission	confusion	intermission	profession
commission	decision	invasion	revision
conclusion	division	omission	supervision
concussion	extension	permission	transfusion
confession	impression	possession	transmission

1. After his ninth explanation of the difference between long and short _____ during the arithmetic lesson, Miguel wondered why he had ever considered teaching to be a worthy _____.

2. Because the teenager was a minor, he was not able to receive the necessary blood _____ until the doctor had obtained _____ from one of his parents.

3. Having completed their survey, the _____ appointed by the governor to study eating patterns came to the sad _____ that people would rather complain about their health than actually do anything about it.

4. In the mass _____ during the fire drill, Dave lost his prize _____, a pocket watch which his uncle had given him for his birthday.

5. Jerome was under the _____ that the carpenters would have the _____ to the living room completed in time for his daughter's wedding, but he was wrong.

6. "Now I've heard everything!" exclaimed the English teacher when one of her students explained that he had not completed the _____ of the composition because, while doing his homework, he had tapped his pencil on his head so often that he was now suffering from a mild _____.

7. The evening after the advertisement appeared in the newspaper announcing that the price of _____ had been reduced to five dollars, there was such an _____ of eager moviegoers that the manager had to turn hundreds of disappointed people away.

8. The organist was so upset over the _____ of his name from the concert program that he stormed out of the theater during the _____.

9. Under the _____ of the tough, new chief of detectives, the investigating team finally got Ms. Tran to sign a _____ in spite of her claim that she was just an innocent victim of circumstances.

10. When the man at Solly's Garage told Ms. Hood that her station wagon needed a brand-new _____, she was confronted with the _____ about whether to have the car fixed or shop around for a new one.

5 More Serious Problems of the Digestive System. A lot can go wrong with the digestive system. Many common conditions are mild and easily treated. But some digestive disorders can be life threatening. What follows are a few of the more serious digestive problems and some common symptoms and treatments for each one. Use the chart to answer the questions that follow.

Condition	Description	Symptoms	Treatment
Appendicitis	Appendicitis is a swelling and redness of the appendix. Bacteria infect the appendix, causing it to fill with pus and swell. The appendix can burst, sending bacteria into the abdomen.	Pain that starts above or around the belly button. Pain can be mild to severe. In time, the pain moves to the right corner of the abdomen and becomes more severe.	Appendicitis is treated by removing the appendix. If left untreated, appendicitis can be fatal.
Diverticulitis	Areas of the inner layer of the large intestines bulge out through the outer muscular wall. The bulges often become walled off and infection sets in.	Fever and pain in the lower left side of the abdomen.	Antibiotics are given to fight the infection, and the person must not eat or drink for a short period of time to rest the intestines.
Gallstones	Gallstones are solid, crystal-like deposits that form in the gallbladder. They can cause the gallbladder to become red and swollen. Gallstones can vary in size from as small as a grain of salt to as large as a golf ball.	A gallbladder attack includes pain that begins in the gut and then moves to the chest and back. It can also include chills and sweating.	Small gallstones may pass out of the body without help. Chronic stones or larger stones may require surgical removal of the gland.
Ulcers	A digestive ulcer is any sore in the lining of the stomach or lower esophagus. Before the 1980s, doctors thought ulcers were caused by stress and too much stomach acid. Today, we know ulcers are caused by bacteria that can live in the digestive tract and weaken the lining.	Heartburn, weight loss, and stomach pain. The stomach pain can be dull or aching.	Treatment includes antibiotics to kill off the bacteria and medicines to reduce the amount of stomach acids.

1. What symptom might indicate that you have appendicitis?

   _____

2. What could happen if you have appendicitis and you do not get treatment?

   _____

   _____

3. If you have pain on the left side of your abdomen, what serious digestive disorder could be the cause?

   _____

4. What symptoms might indicate that there is a problem with your gallbladder?

   _____

   _____

5. If you have frequent, severe gallbladder attacks, what do you think the doctor will do to treat you?

   _____

   _____

6. Does stress cause ulcers? If no, then what does?

   _____

   _____

7. What do the treatments for ulcers and diverticulitis have in common?

   _____

8. What do appendicitis and ulcers have in common?

   _____

What about you?

Write about a common or serious digestive problem that you have or have had in the past. What did you do to fix the problem? Did you take medicine or make changes in your lifestyle? If you have not had any digestive problems or do not want to write about yourself, then write about someone you know.

_____

_____

_____

_____

_____

Are there any changes you and your family could make to increase your digestive health?

_____

_____

_____

_____

_____

6 Word Review. Underline the word in each line that best relates to the first word. Study the example before you begin.

1. **ocean:**	Red	Huron	<u>Pacific</u>	Mediterranean
2. **Colorado:**	country	state	city	Asia
3. **eagerness:**	camel	beaver	gopher	peacock
4. **debt:**	CIA	FBI	IOU	IRS
5. **stomach:**	coma	ulcer	bone	itchiness
6. **disease:**	mumps	heartburn	pimples	freckles
7. **orchard:**	bananas	strawberries	cherries	watermelons
8. **intestines:**	digest	chew	swallow	waste
9. **artist:**	easel	profit	applause	signature
10. **soldier:**	chuckhole	pothole	peephole	foxhole
11. **satellite:**	moon	star	meteor	planet
12. **fuel:**	water	mealtime	oil	cell
13. **19th century:**	1700s	1800s	1900s	2000s
14. **greed:**	Aesop	Pan	Apollo	Midas
15. **aid:**	bother	annoy	help	harm

Words for Study

Tribune	pajamas	viciously	masculine
maximum	utensils	mechanically	masculinity
indifference	gleefully	unnaturally	showoff
Colonel McCormick	exasperated	oppression	sausages
automatic	outraged	frustration	possessive
emphasis	abruptly	comically	necessarily

LESSON 18
A Breakfast Scene

In this lesson, you will read a scene from a famous American play entitled *A Raisin in the Sun* which offers us a picture of one American family at breakfast.

Walter: Something the matter with you this morning?

Ruth: No—I'm just sleepy as the devil. What kind of eggs you want?

Walter: Not scrambled. *(Ruth starts to scramble eggs.)* Paper come? *(Ruth points impatiently to the rolled up Tribune on the table, and he gets it and spreads it out and vaguely reads the front page.)* Set off another bomb yesterday.

Ruth: *(Maximum indifference)* Did they?

Walter: *(Looking up)* What's the matter with you?

Ruth: Ain't nothing the matter with me. And don't keep asking me that this morning.

Walter: Ain't nobody bothering you. *(Reading the news of the day absently again)* Say Colonel McCormick is sick.

Produced by Cleveland Play House, Arizona Theatre Company, and Penumbra Theatre Company. Direction by Lou Bellamy. Franchelle Steward Dorn (Lena) and David Alan Anderson (Walter Lee). Photo by Peter Jennings.

Ruth: *(Affecting tea-party interest)* Is he now? Poor thing.

Walter: *(Sighing and looking at his watch)* Oh, me. *(He waits)* Now what is that boy doing in that bathroom all this time? He just going to have to start getting up earlier. I can't be being late to work on account of him fooling around in there.

Ruth: *(Turning on him)* Oh, no he ain't going to be getting up no earlier no such thing! It ain't his fault that he can't get to bed no earlier nights 'cause he got a bunch of crazy good-for-nothing clowns sitting up running their mouths in what is supposed to be his bedroom after ten o'clock at night…

Walter: That's what you mad about, ain't it? The things I want to talk about with my friends just couldn't be important in your mind, could they?

(He rises and finds a cigarette in her handbag on the table and crosses to the little window and looks out, smoking and deeply enjoying this first one.)

Ruth: *(Almost matter-of-factly, a complaint too automatic to deserve emphasis)* Why you always got to smoke before you eat in the morning?

Walter: *(At the window)* Just look at 'em down there…Running and racing to work…*(He turns and faces his wife and watches her a moment at the stove, and then, suddenly)* You look young this morning, baby.

Ruth: *(Indifferently)* Yeah?

Walter: Just for a second—stirring them eggs. It's gone now—just for a second it was—you looked real young again. *(Then, drily)* It's gone now—you look like yourself again.

Ruth: Man, if you don't shut up and leave me alone.

Walter: *(Looking out to the street again)* First thing a man ought to learn in life is not to make love to no colored woman first thing in the morning. You all some evil people at eight o'clock in the morning.

(Travis appears in the hall doorway, almost fully dressed and quite wide awake now, his towels and pajamas across his shoulders. He opens the door and signals for his father to make for the bathroom in a hurry.)

Travis: *(Watching the bathroom)* Daddy, come on!

(Walter gets his bathroom utensils and flies out to the bathroom.)

Ruth: Sit down and have your breakfast, Travis.

Travis: Mama, this is Friday. *(Gleefully)* Check coming tomorrow, huh?

Ruth: You get your mind off money and eat your breakfast.

Travis: *(Eating)* This is the morning we supposed to bring fifty cents to school.

Ruth: Well, I ain't got no fifty cents this morning.

Travis: Teacher say we have to.

Ruth: I don't care what teacher say. I ain't got it. Eat your breakfast, Travis.

Travis: I am eating.

Ruth: Hush up now and just eat!

(The boy gives her an exasperated look for her lack of understanding, and eats grudgingly.)

Travis: You think Grandmama would have it?

Ruth: No! And I want you to stop asking your grandmother for money, you hear me?

Travis: *(Outraged)* Gaaaleee! I don't ask her, she just gimme it sometimes!

Ruth: Travis Willard Younger—I got too much on me this morning to be—

Travis: Maybe Daddy—

Ruth: Travis!

(The boy hushes abruptly. They are both quiet and tense for several seconds.)

Travis: *(Presently)* Could I maybe go carry some groceries in front of the supermarket for a little while after school then?

Ruth: Just hush, I said. *(Travis jabs his spoon into his cereal bowl viciously, and rests his head in anger upon his fists.)* If you through eating, you can get over there and make up your bed. *(The boy obeys stiffly* *and crosses the room, almost mechanically, to the bed and more or less carefully folds the covering. He carries the bedding into his mother's room and returns with his books and cap.)*

Travis: *(Sulking and standing apart from her unnaturally)* I'm gone.

Ruth: *(Looking up from the stove to inspect him automatically)* Come here. *(He crosses to her and she studies his head.)* If you don't take this comb and fix this here head, you better! *(Travis puts down his books with a great sigh of oppression, and crosses to the mirror. His mother mutters under her breath about his "stubbornness.")* 'Bout to march out of here with that head looking just like chickens slept in it! I just don't know where you get your stubborn ways… And get your jacket, too. Looks chilly out this morning.

Travis: *(With conspicuously brushed hair and jacket)* I'm gone.

Ruth: Get carfare and milk money—*(Waving one finger)*—and not a single penny for no caps, you hear me?

Travis: *(With sullen politeness)* Yes'm.

(He turns in outrage to leave. His mother watches after him as in his frustration he approaches the door almost comically. When she speaks to him, her voice has become a very gentle tease.)

Ruth: *(Mocking; as she thinks he would say it)*

Oh, Mama makes me so mad sometimes, I don't know what to do! *(She waits and continues to his back as he stands stock-still in front of the door.)* I wouldn't kiss that woman good-bye for nothing in this world this morning! *(The boy finally turns around and rolls his eyes at her, knowing the mood has changed and he is vindicated; he does not, however, move toward her yet.)* Not for nothing in this world! *(She finally laughs aloud at him and holds out her arms to him and we see that it is a way between them, very old and practiced. He crosses to her and allows her to embrace him warmly but keeps his face fixed with masculine rigidity. She holds him back from her presently and looks at him and runs her fingers over the features of his face. With utter gentleness.)* Now—whose little old angry man are you?

Travis: *(The masculinity and gruffness start to fade at last)* Aw gaalee, Mama…

Ruth: *(Mimicking)* Aw-gaaaaalleeeee, Mama! *(She pushes him, with rough playfulness and finality, toward the door)* Get on out of here or you going to be late.

1 About the Scene. Answer the following questions in good sentence form.

1. Describe Ruth's relationship with her husband, Walter. Be sure to include details from the scene to support your description.

_____

_____

_____

_____

2. Describe Ruth's relationship with her son, Travis. Be sure to include details from the scene to support your description.

_____

_____

_____

_____

3. Imagine that you are the director of *A Raisin in the Sun*. Describe the type of actress you would be looking for to play the part of Ruth.

_____

_____

_____

_____

4. "A Breakfast Scene" is taken from the first act of *A Raisin in the Sun*, which is a three-act play. Based on what you've read, do you think Walter and Ruth will live "happily ever after," or do you think their marriage will fall apart? Again, include details and reasons to explain your answer.

_____

_____

_____

_____

2 Food for Thought. Foods and sources of food have given our language many interesting slang terms and expressions. Use your common sense and imagination to answer the following questions. The dictionary may be of help to you for some of these terms and expressions.

1. Which of the following is known for being a brainy person who has many ideas?_____.
   a. bonehead   **b.** cabbage head   **c.** egghead   **d.** meathead

2. When the boss calls you into the office to scold you for your latest mistake, he is _____.
   a. biting off more than he can chew   **c.** chewing the rag
   b. chewing the fat   **d.** chewing you out

3. Who would be most likely to ham it up?_____.
   a. a freeloader   **b.** a scatterbrain   **c.** a showoff   **d.** a wallflower

4. Which score indicates that the Detroit Lions made mincemeat out of the St. Louis Rams?_____.
   a. 7–0   **b.** 7–6   **c.** 42–34   **d.** 49–6

5. If you tell a secret to a friend and you don't want him to tell anyone else, you might tell him not to _____.

  a. go bananas   **b.** spill the beans   **c.** upset the apple cart   **d.** stuff sausages

6. "Don't you ever have anything besides rabbit food for lunch?" Marsha complained to her husband. Marsha's husband was in the habit of eating _____ for lunch.

  a. salad   **b.** rabbit stew   **c.** wood shavings   **d.** grass

7. "Sorry I'm late, but it's like pea soup out there," explained Mr. Weaver. Mr. Weaver was referring to _____.

  a. a hailstorm   **c.** a thick fog

  b. a traffic jam   **d.** slippery road conditions

8. Which phrase means the same thing as the expression "in a jam"?_____.

  a. in a pickle   **b.** in a pig's eye   **c.** in the gravy   **d.** out to lunch

9. Which expression would you be most likely to hear from a happy person who has a positive outlook on life?_____.

  a. Butter wouldn't melt in your mouth.   **c.** If life hands you a lemon, make lemonade.

  b. Don't cry over spilled milk.   **d.** You can't have your cake and eat it too.

10. Aunt Betty always said that when you hear gossip, you should just _____.

  a. use your noodle   **c.** stew in your own juice

  b. cry over spilt milk   **d.** take it with a grain of salt

11. My grandfather liked to talk about his salad days because they were the _____.

  a. worst days of his life   **c.** best days of his youth

  b. only times he was happy   **b.** days he remembered best

12. Uncle Anthony had to fire the teenager who worked at his bakery because he said he was not worth his salt. The teenager _____.

  a. stole from him   **c.** did not do a good job

  b. was angry   **d.** treated people poorly

13. If the magazine was selling like hot cakes, the publisher might have to _____.

  a. print more copies   **b.** hose them off   **c.** recycle them   **d.** go out of business

14. The breadwinner in the family is the one who _____.

  a. brings home the bacon   **c.** spills the beans

  b. lives high off the hog   **d.** takes the cake

Language experts have offered explanations for how some of these terms and expressions have entered our everyday speech. For example, one explanation is offered for an expression that appears in Question 14: At many county fairs, the winner of the greased pig event is allowed to bring home the pig as his prize. Which of the four answer choices in Question 14 best matches this explanation? _____

3 Synonyms and Antonyms. Choose a synonym to fill in the first blank in each sentence. Choose an antonym to fill in the second blank. Study the example before you begin.

Synonyms
affection
broad
comical
common
exasperated
extend
extract
gleeful
✓introduction
masculine
minimum
sudden

Antonyms
compress
✓conclusion
contented
dejected
dislike
feminine
infrequent
insert
maximum
narrow
slow
tragic

1. Beginning and ___*introduction*___ are antonyms for ___*conclusion*___.

2. Abrupt and _____ are antonyms for _____.

3. Fondness and _____ are antonyms for _____.

4. Frustrated and _____ are antonyms for _____.

5. Funny and _____ are antonyms for _____.

6. Least and _____ are antonyms for _____.

7. Lengthen and _____ are antonyms for _____.

8. Manly and _____ are antonyms for _____.

9. Merry and _____ are antonyms for _____.

10. Remove and _____ are antonyms for _____.

11. Frequent and _____ are antonyms for _____.

12. Wide and _____ are antonyms for _____.

4 More Work with the Plural Possessive. Because not all plural words in our language end in *s*, it is necessary to learn one more rule for forming plural possessives.

When the plural word does *not* end in *s*, and you want to indicate ownership, add an *'s* to the word just as you do to form the singular possessive. *Women's* and *oxen's* are two examples of this rule.

Use this rule and the other two rules you have studied to form the possessive forms of the words below. Study the examples in order to help you complete this exercise correctly.

Singular	Singular Possessive	Plural	Plural Possessive
1. cereal	cereal's	cereals	cereals'
2. frontiersman		frontiersmen	
3. thief		thieves	
4. foreigner		foreigners	
5. utensil		utensils	
6. child		children	
7. McCormick		McCormicks	
8. Congresswoman		Congresswomen	
9. polisher		polishers	
10. watermelon		watermelons	
11. handyman		handymen	
12. district		districts	
13. reservation		reservations	
14. axman		axmen	
15. deer		deer	

5 The Suffixes -*ance* and -*ence*. One of the most troublesome spelling decisions for many of us is whether to end certain words with -*ance* or -*ence*. Choose the word that best completes each sentence, and write it in the blank. Watch your spelling!

1. In "A Breakfast Scene" the _____ of Walter's son indicates that the bathroom is now free.

    a. attendance   **b.** disobedience   **c.** entrance   **d.** obedience

2. In "A Breakfast Scene" Travis's _____ is evident when his mother refuses to give him money which the teacher has asked the children to bring in.

   a. annoyance **b.** disobedience **c.** importance **d.** independence

3. Because of a certain _____ in eggs, many physicians encourage their patients to cut down on the number they eat each week, while other physicians contend that eggs are one of our most perfect foods.

   a. annoyance **b.** appearance **c.** disturbance **d.** substance

4. Diet experts find it tragic that many Americans prefer _____ foods, which can be prepared and eaten in a hurry, rather than healthful foods, which often require more time to prepare and consume.

   a. convenience **b.** excellence **c.** preference **d.** reference

5. The food industry often counts on public _____ of good diet practices in order to sell their products.

   a. admittance **b.** dependence **c.** ignorance **d.** insistence

6. For example, recognizing the _____ of breakfast but not giving themselves enough time to eat it, many busy Americans gulp down an instant breakfast drink before dashing off to work or school.

   a. dependence **b.** importance **c.** excellence **d.** innocence

7. In gulping down these sweet and tasty breakfast treats, consumers are disobeying the health practice of many diet experts: _____ of sugar.

   a. avoidance **b.** convenience **c.** influence **d.** occurrence

8. By almost everyone's standards, a poor diet lowers _____ to colds and other illnesses that may be going around.

   a. entrance **b.** independence **c.** innocence **d.** resistance

9. Some consumers have lost _____ in the food industry not only because of how food is sold, but also because of the way it is grown.

   a. endurance **b.** confidence **c.** independence **d.** obedience

10. The farmers' attitude may be one of "good _____" as they spray their fields with insecticides to protect their crops from pests, but this is not necessarily an intelligent attitude.

    a. annoyance **b.** resistance **c.** riddance **d.** substance

Words for Study

goulash	ingredients	bok choy	salmon
shish kebabs	pecans	landscape	tortillas
textures	maize	harvest	tofu
aromas	barley	Tex-Mex	pretzels
region	yams	Cajun	baklava

LESSON 19
American Food

Here's a good question: What do you think of when someone says "American Food?" Does pepperoni pizza come to mind? What about hamburgers and French fries? Would you consider goulash American food? How about shish kebabs? American food is as varied as the cultures of the people who live here and the parts of the country that they live in. It is and always has been an ever-changing feast of tastes, textures, and aromas—all brought to life by the mixing of old and new, known and unknown. Even going farther back than when the first settlers came to the New World, American food has always had a life of its own.

Before the Pilgrims arrived—or even Columbus—Native Americans across what is now the U.S. already had cooking styles that varied greatly from region to region. That was due in part to the fact that the same ingredients were not found in every place. Deer might be plentiful in one region, but

goat was the main meat in another. On the East coast, tribes enjoyed blue crab, while along the Northwest coast, tribes ate giant crabs. In New York's Finger Lakes region, eels were commonly eaten.

Native Americans had at least 2,000 different plant foods that they used in their cooking. These included wild celery, sweet potatoes, white potatoes, and turnips. These, too, varied by region. Fruits eaten included strawberries, blueberries, plums, and cherries. Native Americans also ate many different kinds of nuts, seeds, and beans such as pecans, chestnuts, walnuts, sunflower seeds, and peanuts and wild rice in southern regions. The grain used most was maize, which is similar to corn today.

Native Americans used a number of cooking methods. Grilling meat or roasting it over an open fire was common. Vegetables were often cooked directly in the ashes of the fire. In the southwest, Native Americans made ovens to bake items such as breads made from cornmeal. In other parts of the country, Native Americans made ovens by digging pits.

When the colonists first came, they brought with them and raised crops that they were familiar with. They cooked the foods that they knew in the ways that they had in England. Thanks in part to trade with England, the colonists were able to farm and cook in this fashion. Colonists soon learned to eat like Native Americans. They ate a lot of sweet potatoes, maize, berries, and nuts. They also hunted and ate the wild animals of their regions. But instead of cooking over open fires like the Native Americans did, they cooked over fireplaces.

By the 1700s, more settlers from Europe had arrived in the New World. They brought wheat and barley with them to make into flour for bread. Early settlers did not keep animals. But as more settlers came, it got harder and harder to find enough wild deer and other animals to hunt. Spanish settlers in Florida and Dutch and English settlers in the north brought sheep to the New World. Settlers also brought pigs. They began keeping such animals as a way to be sure they would have enough meat. They smoked the pork to make ham and bacon. They also kept chickens for eggs and meat.

American food changed even more quickly in the 1800s. People from all over the world began coming to America. This was especially true for immigrants from Europe, Africa, and China. More ingredients, cooking methods, and recipes came with each new group. From Africa, people brought yams and black-eyed peas. From Europe came noodles, pies, cakes, and vegetables such as lettuce and peas. Hotdogs are based on German sausages. And pizza came to the U.S. with the Italian settlers. Rice, and vegetables such as bok choy, came with the Chinese.

Immigrants introduced—and continue to introduce—new foods to the ever-changing food landscape of this country. But what is even more important is that the ingredients that the foods were made from were now able to be used across cultures, regions, and with already present ingredients to create new foods.

One of the biggest changes in American food came in the 1900s. That's when the use of oil engines and machines came onto the food scene. Oil engines made possible the use of machines to plant and harvest food. They also made it much easier to process food. Oil engines led to canned food and refrigerators. And trains made it possible for fresh milk and vegetables to be brought to cities year-round. Fresh foods of any type from any region could now go to anywhere from anywhere in the country.

Today, the foods of the Northeast have been heavily influenced by the foods eaten by the original colonists. The foods of the South have been heavily influenced by immigrants from Africa, France, and Mexico. Asian cooking has also played a large role in the mixing of food styles in the U.S. Food styles such as Tex-Mex mix the regional food styles of Texas and Mexico. The Pennsylvania Dutch eat the foods of the country's early German settlers. There's Cajun, Southwestern—the list goes on and on. American food continues to change with each new immigrant group that arrives.

But some things have changed very little. Would you be surprised to know that most of the crops grown in the U.S. are the same ones grown before Europeans came? It's true. The crops are corn, sunflowers, beans, and potatoes. And many of the fruits and meats people ate before the settlers arrived are the same—turkey, salmon, and blueberries.

How Long Have We Been Eating That?

Have you ever wondered when your favorite foods were first created? Here are a few common foods and the dates when people first began eating them.

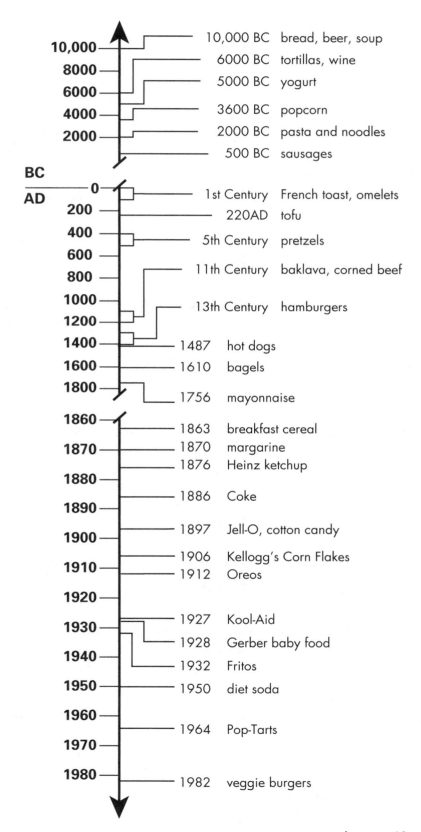

Date	Food
10,000 BC	bread, beer, soup
6000 BC	tortillas, wine
5000 BC	yogurt
3600 BC	popcorn
2000 BC	pasta and noodles
500 BC	sausages
1st Century	French toast, omelets
220AD	tofu
5th Century	pretzels
11th Century	baklava, corned beef
13th Century	hamburgers
1487	hot dogs
1610	bagels
1756	mayonnaise
1863	breakfast cereal
1870	margarine
1876	Heinz ketchup
1886	Coke
1897	Jell-O, cotton candy
1906	Kellogg's Corn Flakes
1912	Oreos
1927	Kool-Aid
1928	Gerber baby food
1932	Fritos
1950	diet soda
1964	Pop-Tarts
1982	veggie burgers

1 About the Reading. Based on the information in the reading, put the letter of the correct answer on the line.

1. Before Columbus, Native American cooking styles _____.
    a. were all alike   **b.** varied greatly   **c.** were kept secret   **d.** were written down

2. On the East coast, tribes enjoyed _____
    a. eels   **b.** giant crab   **c.** blue crab   **d.** bobcat

3. Native Americans across what was to become the U.S. had at least _____ different plant foods that they used in their cooking.
    a. 100   **b.** 2,000   **c.** 20,000   **d.** 1 million

4. Fruits eaten by Native Americans include all of the following except _____.
    a. watermelon   **b.** strawberries   **c.** blueberries   **d.** cherries

5. Instead of cooking over open fires like the Native Americans did, colonists cooked over _____.
    a. open pits   **b.** hot coals   **c.** boiled rocks   **d.** fireplaces

6. Settlers in the 1700s brought wheat and barley with them to make into _____.
    a. flour   **b.** soups   **c.** breakfast   **d.** omelets

7. Settlers smoked _____ to make ham and bacon.
    a. sheep   **b.** pork   **c.** deer   **d.** rabbits

8. One of the biggest changes in American food came in the _____.
    a. 1600s   **b.** 1700s   **c.** 1800s   **d.** 1900s

9. Oil engines led to canned food and _____.
    a. trains   **b.** corn bread   **c.** refrigerators   **d.** Tex-Mex

10. Today, the foods of the Northeast have been heavily influenced by the foods eaten by _____.
    a. the original colonists **b.** the French   **c.** the Italians   **d.** the Germans

11. Immigrants from which of these countries did *not* influence today's foods of the South? _____.
    a. Africa   **b.** France   **c.** Mexico   **d.** Italy

12. The Pennsylvania Dutch eat the foods of what country's early American settlers? _____.
    a. Italian   **b.** French   **c.** German   **d.** Dutch

13. Which of these foods has been around the longest? _____.

    a. tofu   **b.** yogurt   **c.** margarine   **d.** mayonnaise

14. Which of these foods did not exist before the Pilgrims came to America? _____.

    a. tortillas   **b.** bread   **c.** bagels   **d.** pretzels

2 A Taste Test. There are four basic tastes: sweet, salty, bitter, and sour. Classify the food items listed below according to these tastes.

bacon	coffee	hot chocolate	sauerkraut
baking chocolate	coffee cake	lemon peel	smoked ham
cheeseburger	doughnuts	lime juice	soy sauce
cheesecake	grapefruit	mustard greens	vinegar

Sweet

1. _____

2. _____

3. _____

4. _____

Salty

1. _____

2. _____

3. _____

4. _____

Bitter

1. _____

2. _____

3. _____

4. _____

Sour

1. _____

2. _____

3. _____

4. _____

Which of these four tastes is your favorite?

_____

Do you think the food industry has influenced you in preferring this taste? Explain.

_____

_____

_____

3 Word Families. Use the words listed at the left to complete these sentences correctly.

nutrition
nutritious
nutrients

1. Mrs. Chapman thought she was feeding her family _____ meals until she read a book about _____ and realized that her recipes were lacking in many important _____.

entertain
entertainment
entertainer

2. The _____ was tired of spending every weekend providing _____ for others, and he wished someone would come along who would _____ him for a change.

convenience
convenient
conveniently

3. Le loved _____ foods such as TV dinners so much that she _____ forgot her doctor's warning that her stomach did not find a steady diet of this food _____ to manage.

practical
practically
impractical

4. Mr. Lash was _____ finished with the plans for the new shopping mall when he realized that they were so _____ that he'd have to start all over again and come up with a more _____ design.

possessed
possession
possessive

5. Anthony was not normally a _____ person, but he valued his cabin cruiser so much that he would let his friends borrow anything else he _____ just as long as they didn't so much as touch his beloved _____.

confided
confidence
confidential

6. Bart was sure that he was doing the right thing as he told the police officer in a _____ tone of voice the location of the stolen loot which his brother had _____ to him in total _____.

creator
creation
created
creative

7. Standing before the painting in the lobby, the hotel guest exclaimed, "Who _____ this mess!" and then the _____, who just happened to be standing nearby, said sharply, "Madam, the fact that you cannot see this is a wonderful _____ shows that you totally lack a _____ mind!"

obey
obedient
obedience
obediently

8. Mrs. Kraft couldn't understand how her boxer could _____ every single command at _____ school when, at home, he was not at all _____, in spite of the fact that she _____ followed the trainer's instructions.

| science |
| scientist |
| scientific |
| scientifically |

9. "You may be a great _____ who has done much to advance the goals of _____ in our time," snapped Mr. Beaumont at his wife. "But when it comes to _____ managing the family budget, you're about as _____ as a fortune cookie!"

| indifferent |
| indifferently |
| indifference |

10. Filled with _____ about what to eat for supper after a hectic day at work, Tran _____ cracked two eggs into a bowl and was completely _____ to the shocked look on his wife's face as he ate them raw.

4 What Do You Think? Answer the following questions in good sentence form. Be sure to offer support for your answers.

1. Were you surprised to find out that so many different cultural groups helped to form what we call "American food"? Which cultural group and their influence surprised you most? Tell why.

_____

_____

_____

_____

_____

2. What sort of cultural background are you from? Do you have any favorite ethnic dishes from your culture that you enjoy? Describe them. What other ethnic dishes do you like? Describe them and tell why.

_____

_____

_____

_____

_____

5 Can You Crack the Code? Each group of letters on the left spells the name of a jewel, but the name has been concealed by a code in which different letters have been used. The code is the same for all the jewels. When you have guessed a jewel, fill in the letters and use these letters for the other jewels until you have cracked the code for the entire group. Use the facts about the jewels to help you crack the code.

Y D Y G S I U

1. The May birthstone, this gem is a symbol of success. Crunchy Inc. made its green beans look like this beautiful jewel on the label of its cans.

G J C O

2. If Crunchy Inc. started selling beets, they might use the color of this gem for the label. A symbol of safety, the Greeks believed "July children" wearing this jewel could go anywhere and not be harmed.

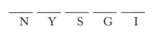
N Y S G I

3. Formed inside the shells of oysters, this gem is soft and can be easily scratched. One of the June birthstones, this jewel is a symbol of health.

U V S D B W U

4. Thousands of years ago, the people in Egypt began the tradition of setting these sparkling jewels in wedding rings. A symbol of love that stays young forever, this gem is the April birthstone.

L B N S A

5. The value of this gemstone depends on its quality. It is a symbol of faithfulness and the November birthstone.

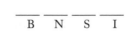
B N S I

6. A symbol of hope, this gem is milky white with a rainbow of colors. It is one of the October birthstones.

F S N N Q V G Y

7. Second only to the diamond in hardness, this gem is sometimes used to make watch crystals. This September birthstone is a symbol of mental and moral well-being.

C I B B U F L B W Y

8. This gem is one of the birthstones for people born in the month of March. It is a symbol of courage.

S D Y L Q O F L

9. The purple color of this gem is believed to be caused by impure substances such as iron. A symbol of being truthful, this jewel is the February birthstone.

K S G W Y L

10. This gem ranges in color from red, brown, and black to different shades of yellow and green. It is a symbol of loyalty and the January birthstone.

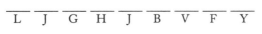
L J G H J B V F Y

11. Many artificial versions of this stone are produced. This bright blue to blue-green stone is the December birthstone and a symbol of wealth.

F S G U B W O P

12. Used in rings and other jewelry, this jewel is one of the cheaper gemstones. One of the August birthstones, it is a symbol of happiness.

6 Review of the Apostrophe. In each sentence, only one of the underlined words needs an apostrophe. Circle that word, and then write it correctly on the line to the left. Sometimes you need to write the singular possessive, and sometimes you need to write the plural possessive. Study the example before you begin.

cents'   **1.** With only fifty <u>cents</u> in his pocket, Junior bought fifty (cents) worth of bubble gum at the candy store.

_____ **2.** As Mrs. Sears prepared the <u>sausages</u> for dinner, she hoped that the <u>sausages</u> taste would be as wonderful as their smell.

_____ **3.** <u>Scientists</u> discoveries are sometimes later regretted by the <u>scientists</u> themselves when they see how people abuse their findings for profit rather than use them for the common good.

_____ **4.** "What do you expect?" said the supervisor to the angry worker. "You work for two <u>days</u>, and you get two <u>days</u> pay."

_____ **5.** When the <u>truckers</u> favorite diner was suddenly invaded by a busload of Girl Scouts, he was sure they were unaware that this particular eating place catered to <u>truckers</u>.

_____ **6.** The <u>warriors</u> confidence was so great that he was able to defeat the enemy <u>warriors</u> despite being outnumbered.

_____ **7.** There were so many <u>Joneses</u> listed in the telephone book that Willy didn't know which of the <u>Joneses</u> numbers to try first.

_____ **8.** Hearing her youngest <u>boys</u> laughter in the next room, Rosella shrugged her shoulders and sighed, "<u>Boys</u> will be <u>boys</u>!"

_____ **9.** Having decided the <u>noodles</u> shape was all wrong for the tuna fish dish she was preparing, Joan returned to the grocery store and bought a package of flat egg <u>noodles</u>.

_____ **10.** The jewelry thief was outraged when he found out that the bracelets he had stolen were not made with real <u>gems</u> and only the <u>gems</u> settings were worth any money.

Words for Study

wizard	miracles	agricultural	presentation
stunningly	transferred	whereas	concocted
cosmetics	Tuskegee	testify	patents
axle	laboratory	Senate	dynamite
remarkable	fulfill	committee	odorless
Missouri	compatibility	snubbed	element

LESSON 20
The Wizard of Alabama

by Peter Tompkins & Christopher Bird

Born sometime during the Civil War, George Washington Carver overcame the handicap of his slave background to be praised in his own lifetime as an outstanding scientist. During a stunningly creative career, Carver turned the lowly peanut, considered useful only as hog food, and the unknown sweet potato into hundreds of separate products, ranging from cosmetics and axle grease to printer's ink and coffee.

From the time he was able to get about by himself in the countryside, young Carver began to display a remarkable knowledge of all growing things. Local farmers in Diamond Grove, a tiny community in southwestern Missouri, remembered the weak-looking boy wandering about for hours, examining plants, and bringing back certain varieties with which he could heal sick animals. Farmers' wives from all over the countryside brought him their ailing house plants, begging him to make them bloom. When he returned the plants to their owners and was asked repeatedly how he could work his miracles, Carver only said softly: "All flowers talk to me and so do hundreds of little living things in the

woods. I learn what I know by watching and loving everything."

Enrolling in a small college in Iowa, Carver supported himself by doing laundry for students. Later he transferred to the Iowa State College of

Agriculture. There his best-loved teacher taught him that nations last only as long as their topsoil. Carrying a heavy load of course work, Carver, a self-taught organist, paid for his education by playing the organ in local churches.

By 1896, Carver had his master's degree and was invited to teach at the college. However, when Booker T. Washington asked him to come to Tuskegee, Alabama, and head his school's department of agriculture, Carver decided to accept. He turned down the well-paying post in Iowa for the opportunity to serve his own people.

Carver had not been in Tuskegee more than a few weeks when he realized that the main problem facing the flat land spreading out in hundreds of square miles around him was its slow poisoning through planting year in year out a single crop—cotton—which for generations had been sucking the life out of the soil. He set up a private laboratory, christened "God's Little Workshop," in which he would sit for hours with plants and into which he never allowed a single book to enter.

For his students at Tuskegee he made his lectures as simple yet as thorough as possible. They were greatly impressed that Carver would rise at four o'clock each morning to walk in the woods before the start of the working day and bring back countless plants for his lectures.

Explaining this habit to friends, Carver said, "Nature is the greatest teacher and I learn from her best when others are asleep. In the still dark hours before sunrise God tells me of the plans I am to fulfill."

The plan Carver fulfilled for which he is perhaps best remembered was his work with the peanut. Late one evening while studying the peanut in his workshop, Carver stared at a peanut plant and asked, "Why did the Lord make you?" In a flash, he received the shortest of answers. "You have three things to go by: compatibility, temperature, and pressure."

With this slim advice. Carver locked himself in his laboratory. There, throughout a sleepless week, he began breaking down the peanut into its parts and exposing them to different conditions of temperature and pressure. Working round the clock, he finally had two dozen bottles, each containing a brand-new product.

Leaving his laboratory, he called a meeting of farmers and agricultural experts and showed them what he had done. He begged his audience to plow under the soil-destroying cotton and plant peanuts instead, telling them that it would produce a cash crop of far more value than its sole existing use as food for pigs might indicate.

The audience was doubtful. To set their minds at ease, Carver began to issue bulletins. In one bulletin, he stated that a rich and healthful butter could be made from the peanut, and that whereas it took one hundred pounds of dairy milk to make ten pounds of butter, a hundred pounds of peanuts could produce thirty-five pounds of peanut butter. Other bulletins showed how many, many products could be extracted from the sweet potato, a vine which most Americans had never heard of.

By 1930, the peanut's one-time worthlessness had been turned into a huge, successful industry, and peanut butter became one of the favorite foods of even the poorest American child. In the middle of the Great Depression, Carver was called to Washington to testify before a Senate committee. Dressed in his usual two-dollar black suit, with an ever-present flower in its buttonhole and a homemade necktie, Carver, upon arriving at Union Station, was snubbed by a waiting porter who, when Carver asked him to help with his bags and direct him to Congress, replied, "Sorry, Pop, I ain't got time for you now. I'm expecting an important colored scientist coming from Alabama." Patiently, Carver carried his own bags to a taxi which took him to Capitol Hill.

The Senate committee had allowed him no more than ten minutes to testify. But when he began his presentation and took from his bag the countless creations concocted in his laboratory, the vice president of the United States overruled the timetable and told Carver he could have as much time as he liked because his presentation was the best that he had ever seen given to a Senate committee.

In half a lifetime of research Carver, though he created fortunes for thousands, rarely made much money from any of his ideas. When people reminded him of the money he might have made had he only protected himself with patents, he replied simply, "God did not charge me or you for making peanuts. Why should I profit from their products?" Thomas Edison told people that "Carver is worth a fortune" and backed up his statement by offering to employ the black scientist at an extremely high salary. Carver turned down the offer. Henry Ford, who thought Carver "the greatest

scientist living," tried to get him to work for him with an equal lack of success.

Because people did not understand the source from which his magic with plant products sprang, they did not understand his methods either. Visitors to his laboratory would find Carver puttering at his workbench cluttered with molds, soils, plants, and insects. The visitors were puzzled by his simple replies to their persistent pleas for him to reveal his secrets.

To one puzzled interviewer, he said: "The secrets are in the plants. To learn them, you have to love them enough."

"But why do so few people have your power?" the man persisted. "Who besides you can do these things?"

"Everyone can," said Carver, "if only they believe it." Tapping a large Bible on a table he added, "The secrets are all here. In God's promises. These promises are real, as real as and more solid than this table."

1 About the Reading. Use information from the reading to complete these statements.

1. George Washington Carver was considered "the wizard from Alabama" because

_____

_____

_____

2. Before Carver's time, Americans did not eat peanuts because

_____

_____

3. Before Carver's time, Americans did not eat sweet potatoes because

_____

_____

4. Carver turned down an offer to teach at Iowa State College because

_____

_____

5. The porter at the train station in Washington, D.C., snubbed Carver because

_____

_____

6. Carver was not interested in making a fortune from his inventions because

_____

_____

_____

7. Cite three examples which indicate that Carver had no particular interest in money.

   a. _____

   b. _____

   c. _____

8. Carver probably called his laboratory "God's Little Workshop" because

_____

_____

_____

9. People were often puzzled by Carver's working methods in his laboratory because

_____

_____

10. Carver believed that anyone could work with plant life the way he himself did if

_____

_____

2 More Facts about the Peanut. Use the words listed below to complete these facts about the peanut correctly.

groundnuts	percent	pods	soil
harvested	period	ripen	temperature
machines	plants	ripened	unusual
pegs	plows	snap	usually

More Facts about the Peanut

The peanut is a fruit of the peanut plant. The peanut is actually a kind of pea, not a nut. Like other peas, peanuts bear seeds in containers called _____. There are _____ two peanuts in each peanut shell. The peanut plant is _____ because its pods grow underground. For this reason, peanuts are often called _____.

Peanut _____ grow best in light, well-drained sandy soil. They need much sunshine, warm _____, and a frost-free growing _____ of four to five months. Farmers must harvest peanuts at the right time. If they harvest their crops too early, many pods will not have _____. If they harvest them too late, the pegs may _____, and many pods will be left in the soil. _____ are the stalk-like stems of the pods.

Most pods _____ 120 to 150 days after planting. At harvest time, farmers use digging _____ to lift the plants from the _____. After they have dried, _____ called combines remove the pods from the plants.

Throughout the world, from 19 to 22 million short tons of peanuts are _____ each year. Farmers in Asia and Africa grow about 85 _____ of the world's peanuts.

3 Word Relationships. On the line, write the letter of the answer that best completes the sentence.

1. Mumps are to illness as _____.
   - **a.** freckles are to nose
   - **b.** lipstick is to cosmetics
   - **c.** orchard is to grove
   - **d.** peanut is to by-product

2. Artificial is to unnatural as _____.
   - **a.** consciousness is to awareness
   - **b.** lecture is to speaker
   - **c.** location is to surrounding
   - **d.** wealth is to well-being

3. Year is to century as _____.
   - **a.** acre is to farmland
   - **b.** cent is to dollar
   - **c.** meter is to centimeter
   - **d.** September is to autumn

4. Melt is to harden as _____.
   - **a.** adapt is to conform
   - **b.** ripen is to harvest
   - **c.** approach is to snub
   - **d.** transform is to transfer

5. Congressman is to Capitol Hill as _____.
   - **a.** organist is to organ
   - **b.** weaver is to blanket
   - **c.** striker is to picket line
   - **d.** scientist is to laboratory

6. Medium is to average as _____.
   - **a.** adventuresome is to restless
   - **b.** convenient is to handy
   - **c.** costly is to impractical
   - **d.** respected is to beloved

7. Grape is to raisin as _____.
   - **a.** juice is to snack
   - **b.** vine is to garden
   - **c.** plum is to prune
   - **d.** lemon is to lemonade

8. Pear is to pare as _____.
   - **a.** eating is to baking
   - **b.** farmer is to cook
   - **c.** fruit is to peeler
   - **d.** knead is to need

9. Natural is to manmade as _____.
   - **a.** wilderness is to settlement
   - **b.** groundnut is to peanut
   - **c.** pigtail is to wig
   - **d.** steer is to dairy cow

10. Plant is to uproot as _____.
   - **a.** combine is to tractor
   - **b.** create is to advertise
   - **c.** fulfill is to transform
   - **d.** restrain is to unleash

4 The Suffix -ize. Use the words below to complete the sentences correctly.

alphabetized	memorize	recognize	symbolize
authorized	modernize	scandalized	tenderized
criticize	organized	specialize	terrorized

1. Joan decided to _____ in the care of babies and young children at medical school after she had a lengthy discussion with her advisor.

2. Mr. Crane finally realized that if he didn't _____ the outdated machinery in his factory, he would probably have to shut down the plant before the end of the year.

3. Even though Kitty had _____ the beef according to the directions, the roast still tasted like shoe leather.

4. For many people, turkey and pumpkin pie _____ the meaning of Thanksgiving more than actually giving thanks.

5. "I expect you to _____ all fifty state capitals by Wednesday," announced Mr. Chapman to his disbelieving geography class.

6. Even Skip's mother-in-law didn't _____ him after his hair transplant that made him look twenty years younger.

7. "Tomorrow I've got to get _____," Johnny muttered to himself upon surveying the pile of dirty laundry in the equally dirty bathroom.

8. "The family will be _____!" said Betsy upon hearing that Uncle Jay had been arrested for driving in circles on the railroad tracks at two o'clock in the morning.

9. The townspeople were _____ by widespread reports that a mob of gangsters was planning to set up headquarters at the local hotel.

10. When the salesclerk said that he wasn't _____ to accept personal checks, the angry customer demanded to see the manager at once.

11. Helen was thankful for the _____ list of recipes in the back of her cookbook whenever she wanted to try out a new casserole.

12. "Praise a child seven times a day; _____ only once" was a piece of advice Mrs. Peck tried to follow whenever she was tempted to speak to her children harshly.

5 Find This Peanut Product. As you learned in the reading, peanuts are used for many products besides peanut butter. Believe it or not, peanuts can not only fill you up, they can blow you up. To find out how, follow these directions for solving the puzzle.

- Fill in the answers to the definitions by using all the syllables in the box. Use each syllable only once.

- The number after each definition tells you how many syllables are in the word.

- The number of letters in each answer is indicated by the number of blank spaces. Study the example before you begin.

- When the words are correctly filled in, their first letters, reading down, will reveal the name of a peanut product which is used to make one of the substances in dynamite.

a	car	di	fu	gurt	ide	lax	ox	rip	tion	✓tril	yo
blad	cord	ex	gall	hale	in	na	ox	sin	tive	vel	
bon	der	fec	gen	hale	in	✓nos	rai	sion	trans	y	

<u>n</u> <u>o</u> <u>s</u> <u>t</u> <u>r</u> <u>i</u> <u>l</u>

__ __ __ __ __ __

__ __ __ __ __ __ __ __ __ __

__ __ __ __ __ __ __

__ __ __ __ __ __

__ __ __ __ __ __ __ __ __ __ __

__ __ __ __ __ __ __ __ __

__ __ __ __ __ __

__ __ __ __ __ __   __ __ __ __ __ __ __

__ __ __ __ __ __

__ __ __ __ __ __

__ __ __ __ __ __ __ __ __ __

__ __ __ __ __ __

1. either of the two outer openings of the nose (2)

2. to breathe in (2)

3. the direct injection of whole blood or another solution into the bloodstream (3)

4. a cord pulled to release the pack of a parachute (2)

5. a colorless, odorless, tasteless element necessary for breathing (3)

6. where bile is stored in your body (3)

7. a drug often taken by people who suffer from constipation (3)

8. a healthful food prepared from milk curdled by bacteria (2)

9. a colorless, odorless gas formed during breathing (5)

10. to breathe out (2)

11. a dried, sweet grape (2)

12. the invasion of a part of the body by germs (3)

13. a synonym for belly button (2)

What is the name of this explosive peanut product?

<u>n</u> __ __ __ __ __ __ __ __ __ __ __

6 To Look at Any Thing. Read the poem. Then answer the questions that follow in good sentence form.

To Look at Any Thing
    by John Moffitt

To look at any thing,
If you would know that thing,
You must look at it long:
To look at this green and say
I have seen spring in these
Woods,' will not do—You must
Be the thing you see:
You must be the dark snakes of
Stems and ferny plumes of leaves,
You must enter in
To the small silences between
The leaves,
You must take your time
And touch the very peace
They issue from.

1. According to the poet, how do most of us see the world around us?

_____

_____

2. According to the poet, what must we do to really know a thing?

_____

_____

_____

3. Cite an example from the reading which indicates that George Washington Carver practiced the advice that the poet offers.

_____

_____

4. Based on the reading, what would George Washington Carver say that we must do in addition to following the poet's advice if we really want to know a thing?

_____

_____

Review: Lessons 1-20

1 Word Review. Use the words listed below to fill in the blanks.

agriculture	frontier	nutrient	profession	transmission
bureau	inflation	patent	Senate	utensil
compatibility	miracle	preservative	tradition	wizard

_____ **1.** a chemical used in foods to prevent spoilage

_____ **2.** a grant made by a government to an inventor, securing him the sole right to make, use, and sell his invention for a certain period of time

_____ **3.** a skillful or clever person; a magician; a male witch

_____ **4.** a substance in food that is necessary for life and growth

_____ **5.** an event that cannot be explained by the laws of nature and so is believed to be supernatural or an act of God

_____ **6.** an occupation requiring training and advanced study in a specialized field

_____ **7.** any instrument or container, especially one used in a kitchen or on a farm

_____ **8.** any unusual increase in available money beyond the amount of available goods, resulting in a sharp and continuing rise in price levels

_____ **9.** land just beyond or at the edge of a settled area; a border between two countries or the area along it

_____ **10.** a specialized government department

_____ **11.** the ability to live or act peacefully

_____ **12.** the gears and related parts of an automobile by which power is sent from the engine to a driving axle; a system of gears

_____ **13.** the passing down of elements of a culture from generation to generation

_____ **14.** the science, art, and business of planting crops and raising livestock useful to man

_____ **15.** the upper house of Congress in the United States to which two members are elected from each state by popular vote for a six-year term

2 Which Word Does Not Fit? Choose the word that does not fit with the rest of the words in each line and write it to the right.

1. pajamas	bathrobe	slippers	nightgown	windbreaker	_____
2. save	deserve	reserve	store	preserve	_____
3. numb	edgy	nervous	tense	upset	_____
4. Arctic	Indian	Pacific	Atlantic	Mediterranean	_____
5. crisis	crossroad	emergency	starvation	zero hour	_____
6. honor	praise	applause	salary	compliment	_____
7. Rome	Paris	Moscow	Warsaw	Los Angeles	_____
8. loyal	dutiful	faithful	obedient	hardworking	_____
9. curb	limit	reject	confine	restrain	_____
10. plague	sorrow	distress	suffering	heartbreak	_____
11. clever	valued	creative	skilled	resourceful	_____
12. secret	unknown	stunning	mysterious	unexplained	_____
13. apple	peach	turnip	grapefruit	raspberry	_____
14. Adams	Jackson	Kennedy	Franklin	Lincoln	_____
15. gold	opal	topaz	turquoise	amethyst	_____

3 Word Study. Use the words listed at the left to complete these sentences.

emergency
endure
nagging
plagued
immediately

1. _____ by a _____ toothache, Terry could no longer _____ the pain, so she _____ phoned the dentist for an _____ appointment.

authorize
classified
creative
opportunities
outraged

2. Hiram was so _____ when his boss refused to _____ his latest project that he began to check the _____ ads for more _____ employment _____.

assistant
assumed
concocted
explanation
scientist

3. The _____ _____ that the solution he'd _____ in his laboratory would still be there the following morning, but it had strangely disappeared, and his _____ could offer no helpful _____

advice
advised
device
devise
revise

4. "Take my _____ and _____ a less costly method for producing this _____," _____ Ms. Franklin's supervisor, "or I'll have to _____ the entire budget for your project."

desperate
dutiful
foul
injected
oppression

5. So _____ were the formerly _____ servants to put an end to the King's _____ that they _____ poison in the roast being prepared for his supper, hoping that he would not suspect _____ play.

confident
detract
envy
formally
formerly

6. When he was _____ appointed stage manager, Alexis—who had _____ been "just one of boys"—was _____ that any _____ the other crew members might feel toward him wouldn't _____ from the many friendships he had at the theater.

accommodate
limit
maximum
minimum
resume

7. Because interest in river travel in winter was at a _____, the owners of a steamboat which could _____ a _____ of eighty passengers decided to _____ the number of cruises to two and _____ their regular number of runs in the spring.

unfruitful
unknown
unlike
unpleasant
unusually

8. The board chairman thought it was _____ anything he had ever seen; for some _____ reason, everyone was so _____ that Thursday afternoon that the meeting was not only lengthy but also totally _____.

4 Review of Compound Words. Put the letter of the correct answer on the line to the left.

_____   **1.** Which word is related to the activities of Sally Ride?

     a. handicraft   **b.** spacecraft   **c.** witchcraft   **d.** woodcraft

_____   **2.** What would cause a burglar to think he is being tailed?

     a. doorsteps   **b.** footsteps   **c.** insteps   **d.** sidesteps

_____   **3.** Which word is a synonym for _limelight_?

     a. candlelight   **b.** floodlight   **c.** gaslight   **d.** spotlight

_____   **4.** If you lived on a small island and grew tired of seeing the same old faces, where might you go for a change?

     a. mainland   **b.** mainspring   **c.** mainstay   **d.** mainstream

_____   **5.** Which word is a synonym for _positively_?

     a. downpour   **b.** downswing   **c.** downright   **d.** downturn

_____   **6.** Which word refers to a painted curtain hung at the back of a stage set?

     a. backdrop   **b.** backrest   **c.** backside   **d.** backstage

_____   **7.** What do you call a group of pages made available on the Internet by a person or group?

     a. spider web   **b.** website   **c.** webpage   **d.** webfoot

_____   **8.** Which word describes a temporary lack of consciousness?

     a. blackout   **b.** blowout   **c.** brownout   **d.** whiteout

_____   **9.** Which of the following is a synonym for _disadvantage_ or _inconvenience_?

     a. drawback   **b.** greenback   **c.** humpback   **d.** tailback

_____   **10.** Which word refers to a painful digestive disorder?

     a. hailstone   **b.** gallstone   **c.** limestone   **d.** birthstone

_____   **11.** If your day has run like _____, everything has gone without a hitch.

     a. piecework   **b.** groundwork   **c.** clockwork   **d.** teamwork

_____   **12.** Since you have only two more exercises to complete in this reading book, you could say that you are in the _____.

     a. homecoming   **b.** homeroom   **c.** homestretch   **d.** homework

5 Review of Contractions. Write the contractions for the following words on the lines to the right. Study the example before you begin.

1. he is   **he's** _____

2. they will _____

3. does not _____

4. we have _____

5. you had _____

6. I would _____

7. had not _____

8. will not _____

9. she has _____

10. you will _____

11. do not _____

12. I will _____

13. what is _____

14. they had _____

15. there is _____

16. she would _____

17. I am _____

18. let us _____

19. he had _____

20. madam _____

6 Review of Facts and Opinions. Write *fact* on the line to the left if the statement is a fact. Write *opinion* if the statement is an opinion.

_____ 1. John Quincy Adams was the sixth president of the United States.

_____ 2. Ketchup has been around longer than peanut butter.

_____ 3. Water with lemon tastes better than diet soda.

_____ 4. South Carolina became a state before Missouri did.

_____ 5. South Carolina is a more interesting state to visit than Missouri.

_____ 6. There are more motorists on the highway now than there were twenty-five years ago.

_____ 7. The motorists in Boston have a higher accident rate than the motorists in Salt Lake City.

_____ 8. Some people believe that America's space program is too costly.

_____ 9. More women have been elected to Congress since 1960 than before 1960.

_____ 10. The life of a congresswoman is more difficult than that of a congressman.

_____ 11. Several lessons in this reading book have offered advice about getting a job.

_____ 12. Completing the readings and exercises in this reading book has been a lot of fun.

Answer Key

Lesson 1

1 About the Reading

1. variety
2. obesity
3. grocery stores and refrigerators
4. small meals
5. serving
6. nutrition
7. portion
8. metabolism
9. labels
10. heart
11. a, b, and c
12. prepare

What do you think? Answers will vary. Accept any reasonable response.

2 Which Word Does Not Fit?

1. bakery
2. chain
3. list
4. diseased
5. drinking
6. thing
7. nurse
8. diet
9. mild
10. dentist
11. likely
12. question

3 Spelling

1. sleepiness
2. ugliness
3. dizziness
4. healthiness
5. nastiness
6. loveliness
7. dustiness
8. greasiness
9. holiness
10. fruitiness

4 Reading a Nutrition Label

1. Two Fruit & Nut Oat Bars would total 270 calories.
2. The Fruit & Nut Oat Bar is healthier because the Honey-Nut Raisin Bar has more total fat and sugar.
3. The Fruit & Nut Oat Bar is better for your heart because it has no trans fats.
4. I would choose the Honey-Nut Raisin Bar because it has more protein.
5. The Fruit & Nut Oat Bar is much lower in sodium, so it's better for your blood pressure.
6. The Fruit & Nut Oat Bar has the healthiest carbohydrates because it has more fiber and less sugar.
7. Answers will vary. Sample answer: I would choose the Fruit & Nut Oat Bar because it is lower in calories and has healthy nutrients.
8. Answers will vary. Sample answer: An athlete on a long run or bike ride might want the Honey-Nut Raisin Bar because it has a lot of carbs and protein.

5 Words That End with -ness

1. fondness
2. loudness
3. rudeness
4. forgiveness
5. gracefulness
6. awareness
7. eagerness
8. stillness
9. goodness
10. forgetfulness
11. calmness
12. seriousness

Lesson 2

1 About the Reading

1. The wedding guest is surprised because Benjamin has dark skin and his grandmother has very pale skin.
2. Answers may vary. Sample answer: Benjamin might think that his family is perfectly normal.
3. Answers may vary.
4. The U.S. Census Bureau collects information about the population such as race, ethnicity, employment, and living situation.
5. Answers may vary. Sample answer: New York, Texas, and California have a lot of immigrants. Texas and California are on the Mexican border. New York City is where many immigrants arrived by boat in the 1800s and early 1900s.
6. Answers may vary. Accept any reasonable response.
7. Answers may vary. Accept any reasonable response.
8. Answers may vary. Accept any reasonable response.

2 Where Do They Come From?

1. Africans
2. Americans
3. Asians
4. Canadians
5. Chinese
6. Cubans
7. Egyptians
8. English
9. French
10. Germans
11. Greeks
12. Dutch
13. Hungarians
14. Irish
15. Japanese
16. Koreans
17. Mexicans
18. Nicaraguans
19. Nigerians
20. Norwegians
21. Pacific Islanders
22. Romanians
23. Russians
24. Swedes
25. Swiss

3 Words That End with -ment

1. shipment
2. enlargement
3. engagement
4. measurement
5. commitment
6. ailment
7. management
8. enjoyment
9. advancement
10. encouragement
11. discouragement
12. confinement

4 The Capitol and Capitals

1. Sacramento
2. Denver
3. Tallahassee
4. Honolulu
5. Springfield
6. Topeka
7. Boston
8. Lansing
9. Jackson
10. Trenton
11. Columbus
12. Oklahoma City
13. Columbia
14. Nashville
15. Austin
16. Salt Lake City

Lesson 3

1 About the Reading

1. d
2. b
3. a
4. b
5. c
6. c
7. b
8. d
9. a
10. c
11. d
12. b

2 Synonyms

1. similar	5. unique	9. ability
2. specialist	6. obese	10. separate
3. convenient	7. individual	11. absolute
4. advancement	8. substitute	12. diverse

3 Antonyms

1. separate	5. specialize	9. multiple
2. challenging	6. convenient	10. diverse
3. discouragement	7. fertile	11. obese
4. confinement	8. unusual	12. supersized

4 Spelling

1. thieves	5. leaves	8. selves
2. calves	6. loaves	9. wives
3. elves	7. shelves	10. knives
4. halves		

5 Capitalization Rules: Part 1

1. John, Mary, Cape, Cod, Thousand, Islands
2. On, Fourth, July, Ohio, River
3. Roger, South, America, Africa, Europe
4. Mrs., Price, Christmas, October, Thanksgiving
5. On, Good, Friday, Dr., Lodge, Chestnut, Street
6. When, Kate, Carver, City, Hospital, Riverside, Lane
7. Ruth, Andrew, Jackson, England, Monday
8. Buddy, August, Great, Smoky, Mountains, Dr., Carpenter
9. Mr., Knight, Rosebud, Lane, Columbia, South, Carolina
10. I, I, Honolulu, I, Vermont, Uncle, Steven

Lesson 4

1 About the Story

1. At the beginning of the story, Lisa feels irritated.
2. Grandma Janey is in such a good mood that Lisa cheers up and starts to feel better.
3. Grandma Janey's house is old and dark inside and possibly in need of some repair.
4. Grandma Janey probably dresses up in flashy outfits because it reminds her of her days in the theater.
5. Answers will vary. Accept any reasonable response.
6. Your immune system is like an army that fights off disease. Aging and certain diseases can weaken your immune system.
7. Answers will vary. Accept any reasonable response.
8. Lisa is really worried that her mother will get sick like Grandma Janey when she gets older.
9. Answers will vary. Accept any reasonable response.
10. Answers will vary. Accept any reasonable response.

2 Synonyms

1. exotic	5. assist	9. anxiety
2. fabulous	6. theater	10. costume
3. immune	7. previously	11. elaborate
4. behavior	8. medley	12. scenery

3 Antonyms

1. flashy	5. advance	9. picky
2. usual	6. elaborate	10. slump
3. uneaten	7. broad	11. unknown
4. irritate	8. forget	12. vivid

4 More Work with the Ending -ness

1. freshness	5. dullness	8. truthfulness
2. politeness	6. dryness	9. bitterness
3. smoothness	7. plumpness	10. gentleness
4. stiffness		

5 Spelling

1. thirstiness	5. noisiness	9. scratchiness
2. riskiness	6. nosiness	10. itchiness
3. craziness	7. bloodiness	11. faultiness
4. pickiness	8. flashiness	12. sneakiness

6 Capitalization Rules: Part 2

1. When, Holiday, Inn, Mr., Holland, Greek, Forest, Avenue
2. Adam, Super, Bowl, Dallas, Cowboys
3. Ms., Woods, Huron, Indians, Spring, Valley, Public, Library, Pueblo, Indians
4. When, Ford, Bush, County, Courthouse, Louis, Standard, Savings, Loan
5. The, Free, Ride, Insurance, Company, Dr., Springfield, Rolls, Royce, Roger's, Fish, Market, Perch, Street
6. I, Mr., Brooks, Steven, Coke, Tuesday, War
7. When, Jackson, Washington, D.C., Capitol, Congress
8. While, Tony, Aunt, Martha, Springfield, Falls, Road, Middle, School

Lesson 5

1 About the Reading

1. Low-paying jobs and expensive housing are two reasons that many families are homeless.
2. Answers will vary. Sample answer: Some people might buy a lot of things on credit and then make only minimum payments without realizing how fast the debts add up.
3. Being in debt can make people feel depressed and anxious.
4. Answers will vary. Accept any reasonable response.
5. To lower your electric bill, you can turn off devices you're not using and switch to energy-efficient lightbulbs.
6. Families can save money by buying food in bulk and then freezing it in smaller portions.
7. Families can purchase mis-mixed paint at a discount and recover old furniture to give a room a new look.
8. Answers will vary. Accept any reasonable response.
9. Answers will vary. Accept any reasonable response.

2 Word Families

1. decorator, redecorate, decorations
2. entertainment, entertain
3. capital, capitalize, capitalization
4. assistant, assistance, assist

5. responsible, responsibility, responsibly
6. inconvenient, convenient, convenience
7. multiple, multiples, multiplied
8. persisted, persistent, persistence
9. nutritious, nutrients, nutrition
10. appearance, disappearance, disappeared, appear

3 Capitalization Review

1. the merry month of May
2. a roll of cherry Life Savers
3. 620 Riverside Drive
4. her French book
5. the U.S. Justice Department
6. a can of Coke
7. the University of Iowa
8. the Roaring Twenties
9. a Dodge truck
10. Halloween pranks
11. the Canadian flag
12. the Oklahoma State Fair

4 More Work with the Ending -ment

1. punishment
2. employment
3. requirement
4. involvement
5. retirement
6. wonderment
7. mistreatment
8. government
9. Detachment
10. misplacement
11. concealment
12. consignment

5 Compound Words

1. a
2. d
3. d
4. c
5. a
6. b
7. d
8. d
9. b
10. a
11. d
12. a

Review: Lessons 1–5

1 Word Review

1. metabolism
2. Pilgrims
3. statue
4. Alzheimer's disease
5. identical twins
6. debt
7. convenience store
8. census
9. Capitol
10. Salt Lake City
11. Thomas A. Edison
12. Alaska
13. fertility treatments
14. clearance
15. Andrew Jackson

2 Synonyms and Antonyms

1. synonyms
2. antonyms
3. synonyms
4. antonyms
5. synonyms
6. synonyms
7. antonyms
8. synonyms
9. antonyms
10. synonyms
11. antonyms
12. synonyms
13. synonyms
14. antonyms
15. antonyms

3 Where Might You Find These?

1. theaters
2. Massachusetts
3. Capitol building
4. whole grains
5. drive-through
6. Pennsylvania
7. state capitals
8. Europe
9. Mississippi
10. handbag
11. West Africa
12. Census Bureau
13. pharmacy
14. New York City
15. dairy aisle

4 Suffixes

1. decorator
2. scientist
3. saltiness
4. usefulness
5. efficiency
6. seriously
7. persistence
8. appearance
9. portions
10. challenging

5 Review of Capitalization Rules

Answers will vary.

6 Compound Words

1. checkerboard
2. officeholder
3. leftover
4. underclothes
5. manpower
6. blackjack
7. upbringing
8. sandman
9. oddball
10. hitchhiker
11. inkblot
12. offspring

City: Columbus
State: Ohio

Lesson 6

1 About the Reading

1. b
2. b
3. c
4. a
5. d
6. c
7. a
8. d

2 What Do You Think?

Answers will vary. Accept any reasonable response.

3 Synonyms

1. own
2. uncertain
3. disgraced
4. allow
5. lately
6. frighten
7. relaxed
8. change
9. dejected
10. disperse
11. lesson
12. idea

4 The Suffix -ful

1. scoopful
2. playful
3. eventful, fearful
4. forceful
5. regretful, plateful

5 The Suffix -less

1. shameless
2. heartless
3. ageless
4. meaningless, blameless
5. fearless, mindless

6 Review of Capitalization Rules

1. October, Black, Tuesday, American, Wall, Street, New, York, City
2. During, Depression, Washington, United, States
3. In, Chicago, Illinois
4. In, Uncle, Robert, Campbell's, Ritz
5. Not, Great, Depression, In, Georgia, Black, In, New, York, Indian
6. A, Texas, As, I, I've
7. On, December, Americans, Japanese, Pearl, Harbor, Hawaii, Shortly, Congress, Japan
8. The, Great, Depression, Congress, United, States, World, War

Lesson 7

1 About the Reading

1. d   4. c   7. d
2. a   5. d   8. b
3. a   6. b

An arithmetic problem: 1824

2 Symbols

First set:

1. striped pole   6. ⓘ
2. CO_2 7. scales
3. white cross   8. ♫
4. four-leaf clover   9. skull and crossbones
5. capital H   10. Uncle Sam

Second set:

1. bat   5. dove   8. ox or bull
2. bee or ant 6. eel   9. mule
3. beaver   7. fox   10. owl
4. lamb

3 Word Families

1. election, elected
2. adjustments, adjust
3. reference, refer
4. prefer, preference
5. slippery, slipperiness
6. hearty, heartily, heartless
7. stubborn, stubbornly, stubbornness
8. application, applicant, applied
9. cowardliness, cowardly, coward
10. usual, usually, unusually, unusual

4 Looking for a Job

1. a. Monday
   b. Friday
   c. September
   d. appointment
   e. between
   f. and
2. Bus person at Rolling Hills Country Club
3. Construction "Jack-of-all-Trades" and Manager for ladies' sportswear shop
4. Personal appearance and/or personality are probably important for the job, and the interviewer wants an opportunity to judge these factors.
5. Answers will vary.

5 Can You Crack the Code?

1. James Polk   6. Abraham Lincoln
2. George Washington   7. John Adams
3. John F. Kennedy   8. Thomas Jefferson
4. John Quincy Adams   9. James Madison
5. Andrew Jackson   10. James Monroe

Lesson 8

1 About the Reading

1. You should learn about technology because it is likely to play a major role in job searches in the future.
2. When searching for career advice online, visit well-known career sites.
3. Make sure to send your information in the manner requested. Following directions shows that you are serious about meeting an employer's needs.
4. Always make sure to communicate in a professional manner, no matter how informal a group may seem. Employers sometimes listen in on such discussions.
5. Think twice before posting silly pictures and personal stories online. An employer could stumble across your personal profile.
6. Job seekers looking for flexible employment need to be aware of telecommuting and work-from-home scams, which are fairly common.
7. New opportunities often require new strategies. As technology continues to change, applicants' strategies will also need to shift and adjust.
8. In 2001, most people who had flexible work arrangements were pleased with those arrangements.

2 Antonyms

1. strict   5. casual   9. unfriendly
2. manageable   6. unnecessary 10. limited
3. uneasy   7. imagined   11. warning
4. reject   8. old   12. less

3 Who Does What?

1. alumni   7. telecommuter
2. expert   8. applicant
3. on-call worker   9. social networker
4. freelancer   10. short-term worker
5. scammer   11. commuter
6. blogger   12. potential employer

4 The Suffix -ly

1. d   5. c   8. b
2. c   6. a   9. b
3. b   7. d   10. c
4. d

5 Capitalization Rules: Part 3

1. In, English, Thursday, Mr., Fisher, *A, Tale, Two, Cities*, Monday
2. While, South, Trentons, Stony, Brook, Motel, Beech, Avenue, Memphis
3. Francis, Scott, Key, The, Star-Spangled, Banner, War, British
4. When, Peggy, Hickock, County, *Grand, Island, Daily, Times*
5. Mrs., Ritz, Department, Transportation, Washington, D.C., New, England
6. Upon, Smothers, Business, College, Louise, Mick, Just, Typing, Typing, Walnut, Hills, High, School

7. Mr., East, North, Street, South, Street, West, Branch, Savings, Loan

8. When, Jesse, Christianity, Judaism, Islam, Bible, Talmud, Koran

9. The, American, Red, Cross, Sons, Italy, Moosewood, City, Hall

10. Leafing, *Family*, *Circle*, James, Jefferson, Boston, Helping, Hand, Club's

6 Online Job Advertisement

1. Return to the search results.
   Apply to the job.
   Save the ad.
   E-mail the ad.
   Print the ad.
   Map the directions.
   Find out salary information about the job.

2. A college degree is preferred, but not required for the job.

3. No, you do not manage others.

4. At least 18 hours of related coursework (Education, Early Childhood, Child Development, Psychology, etc.).
   Experience working with children under the age of 6 years.

5. The number of hours you work.
   Your experience.
   Your education.

6. You work with students and their families.

7. The full-time hours are 8:30 a.m.-5:30 p.m., Monday through Friday.
   The part-time hours are 8:30 a.m.-12:30 p.m., Monday through Friday.

8. Answers will vary.

9. The "map it" link would let you map out directions to the job.

7 More Work with the Suffix -*ly*

1. angrily	5. mightily	9. dreamily
2. heartily	6. lazily	10. unworthily
3. merrily	7. steadily	11. guiltily
4. cheerily	8. crazily	12. dizzily

Lesson 9

1 About the Reading

1. c	4. d	7. c
2. d	5. b	8. b
3. a	6. d	

2 Positive and Negative

Answers will vary. Reasonable responses include:

2. *Positive*: Select your outfit carefully, making sure your clothes are clean, neat, and business-like, and that they look good on you.
   Negative: Think, "It really doesn't matter what I wear because I probably won't get the job anyway."

3. *Positive*: Describe clearly the things you do well, any training you have had, and any experience you have that may apply to this particular job.

Negative: Act unsure of what you can do, or say, "I really don't have any experience, but I can probably learn to do most anything."

4. *Positive*: Remember that the interview itself was a good learning experience which will help you to do better the next time.
   Negative: Give up trying to find a job because you know you'll never get one.

3 Work with Classifications

Days	Languages	Measurements
Fri.	Eng.	gal.
Mon.	Fr.	lb.
Sat.	Ital.	oz.
Thurs.	Jap.	pt.
Wed.	Rus.	qt.

States	Months
AL	Aug.
CA	Dec.
MA	Jan.
NY	Mar.
WA	Sept.

4 How Would You Classify This?

1. state	5. skill	9. material
2. quality	6. rule	10. personality
3. income	7. promise	11. technology
4. employee	8. crime	12. manner

5 More Work with the Suffix -*ly*

1. legally	6. useless	11. social
2. positive	7. popularly	12. negatively
3. immediate	8. separately	13. individually
4. fearlessly	9. impolite	14. previously
5. currently	10. useful	15. realistically

6 Filling out an Employment Application

Answers will vary.

Lesson 10

1 About the Story

1. Life seemed "hollow and a burden" because Tom had to paint a fence on a beautiful summer Saturday.

2. He had managed to get other people to pay him to let them paint the fence.

3. Once his tactic had worked on that boy, the rest was easy.

4. Tom was playing "hard to get" and making it seem as though he took pride in the job and enjoyed doing it.

5. The "law of human action" Tom used was that to make someone want something badly, you make it difficult to get.

6. Work is something you have to do, and play is something you don't have to do.

7. Answers will vary. Accept any reasonable response.

8. Answers will vary. Accept any reasonable response.

2 If Only Someone Else Would Do It!

1. dressmaker
2. student
3. teacher
4. floorwalker
5. stationmaster
6. butcher
7. lifeguard
8. treasurer
9. cowboy
10. scribe

Answers will vary on the last two questions.

3 Word Relationships

1. b
2. b
3. a
4. c
5. d
6. d
7. b
8. c
9. d
10. a

4 Review of Suffixes

1. judgment
2. contentment
3. merciless
4. blankness
5. vastly
6. purely
7. scornful
8. vagueness
9. merciful
10. dutiful
11. bareness
12. innocently
13. limitless
14. childless
15. misjudgment

5 Spelling

1. differences
2. lightning
3. possession
4. somebody
5. your
6. starving
7. hundred
8. cabbages
9. can't
10. promise
11. thankful
12. experience

6 What Exactly Is a Jew's Harp?

incorrectly, consists, create, finger

traveled, concerts, damaged, dentist, resume, instrument

Europe, glory, popular, Asia, gentlemen

Review: Lessons 1–10

1 Word Review

1. interview
2. suffix
3. prefix
4. whitewash
5. crisis
6. experiment
7. Mark Twain
8. United Nations
9. felony
10. applicant
11. roll call
12. Abraham Lincoln

2 Word Review

1. d
2. c
3. a
4. d
5. b
6. b
7. a
8. c
9. c
10. a
11. d
12. a

3 Review of Capitalization Rules

Answers will vary.

4 Looking for a Job

1. a. references
   b. transportation
   c. weekly
   d. responsible
   e. preferred
   f. available
   g. company
   h. license
2. 555-3141 and 555-2747
3. It means the position pays an hourly wage, and in addition there is a commission paid on sales made.

4. Any of the following: Baby Sitter Needed; Bar staff, Waitress & Porter; Child Care; Cleaners; Driver; Pet Shop Clerk; Photo Store; Sales Help for Craft Store; Sales-Weekends Pet Shop; Service Agent Position; Telephone Sales; Telephone Sales & Appointments; Typist; Waiters-Waitresses
5. Any of the following: Control Desk Person; Presser; Sales-Weekend Pet Shop; Service Agent Position
6. Equal Opportunity Employer

What do you think? Answers will vary.

5 Find the Quote

1. penknife
2. New Year's Eve
3. positive
4. teakettle
5. Honolulu
6. thirteen
7. lighthouse
8. tadpole
9. Daddy
10. artery
11. engineer
12. wallflower

Quote: The only thing people in every walk of life will agree on is that they are underpaid and overworked.

Compound Words

1. corncob, haystack
2. scatterbrain, airline
3. fiddlesticks, cookout
4. staircase, Checkmate
5. signpost, sideswiped
6. aftertaste, mouthwash
7. waterfront, seasick
8. lifelong, masterpiece

Lesson 11

1 About the Reading

1. a. the barber was stunned.
   b. the captain was unhurt.
   c. he returned to help rescue the wounded.
   d. he begged the others to shoot him.
   e. the wounded were taken to Memphis.
   f. the physicians gave him less attention.
   g. Memphis knew how to respond to the accident.
   h. patients for whom there was no hope were taken to the death room.
   i. the chief mate refused both medicine and water.
   j. he was able to work again as a mate on a steamboat.
2. Answers will vary. Accept any reasonable response.

2 Idle Threats

1. intend, contend, extend, attend
2. preview, review, overview, interview
3. devise, revise, advise, supervise
4. admit, commit, transmit, submit
5. reserve, conserve, deserve, preserve
6. impose, dispose, compose, expose
7. depress, compress, express, impress
8. extract, contract, detract, subtract

3 Traveling by Steamboat

1. cabins
2. There are two formal dinners during the cruise.
3. The boat would stop at the nearest shore stop to get a doctor.

4. your own insurance or travel agent
5. There are only two wheelchair-accessible cabins, so you have to call ahead to make sure you can reserve one.
6. nothing (They are provided by the steamboat company.)
7. on the sun deck
8. any of the following: wine, photographs, gifts
9. The ticket describes the legal contract between the company and the passenger.
10. Answers will vary. Accept any reasonable response.

4 Synonyms and Antonyms

1. moored, adrift
2. naked, clothed
3. abuse, tenderness
4. offspring, ancestors
5. ruin, create
6. compliment, insult
7. unending, passing
8. precisely, vaguely
9. seep, gush
10. faultless, incorrect
11. formerly, currently
12. active, idle

5 Contractions

1. isn't
2. I'm
3. don't
4. doesn't
5. didn't
6. she's
7. it's
8. I'd
9. I'll
10. he'll
11. you're
12. you've

Lesson 12

1 About the Reading

1. d
2. d
3. a
4. b
5. c
6. a
7. a
8. c
9. c
10. d

2 What Do You Think?

Answers will vary.

3 More Work with Contractions

1. we'd
2. they'd
3. she'll
4. he'll
5. we're
6. they've
7. he's
8. how's
9. there's
10. hasn't
11. weren't
12. ma'am

4 Word Relationships

1. disaster is to tragic
2. taut is to slack
3. drill is to dentist's office
4. alter is to revise
5. train is to engine
6. North Carolina is to the South
7. sober is to silly
8. mph is to abbreviation
9. bloom is to wilt
10. airbag is to automobile

5 The Prefix *un-*

1. untrue
2. undesirable
3. uninterested
4. uninformed
5. unfastened
6. unfruitful
7. unexpected
8. unleashed
9. unskilled
10. Unsafe
11. ungrateful
12. unlimited

Lesson 13

1 About the Story

1. d
2. a
3. c
4. b
5. c
6. d
7. a
8. b
9. c
10. a

2 The Apostrophe to Show Ownership

1. Polly's impression
2. the cheerleader's uniform
3. the actress's costume
4. the morphine's effects
5. Mrs. Mack's coffee cake
6. the screenwriter's masterpiece
7. the angel's wings
8. the beekeeper's hives
9. the chief's discovery
10. Jackie's bad temper
11. the earth's atmosphere
12. the psychiatrist's patients

3 A Fat Boy without Any Clothes On

arrows, pierces
wildness, supposed, create, reject
deadly, perched
bowstring, eyes
sprinted, escape, prayed, plea
sorry, crown

4 More Prefixes That Mean *Not*

1. impure
2. indigestion
3. illegal
4. irresponsible
5. inexperience
6. nonmetal
7. independent
8. indirect
9. nonskid
10. Improper
11. Indecent
12. insane
13. Nonsense
14. impatient

5 Money

Answers to both parts of this question will vary. Accept any reasonable responses.

6 More about Money

1. doesn't do anything serious; is silly; wastes time
2. one's fate; one's place in life
3. The poet seems to agree with Anthony Rockwall, because he says that he'd change places with a rich man.
4. Answers will vary.

Lesson 14

1 About the Reading

1. b
2. d
3. d
4. c
5. a
6. b
7. a
8. c
9. d

2 More Work with the Apostrophe

1. the butcher's apron
2. Manhattan's skyline
3. Tony's cousins
4. the Volkswagen's radiator
5. Jack's fractured arm
6. the gerbil's cage
7. Francis's journey
8. Mr. Royal's servants
9. the satellite's orbit
10. the clinic's lounge
11. the veterinarian's routine
12. the angel's halo

3 Understanding Cartoons

1. Sally's role as a woman
2. the noses; because the reporters are being nosy
3. She is angry. This is indicated by the black cloud over her head as she turns her back on them and walks away.
4. The cartoonist seems to be on Sally's side because the reporters' questions are stupid and sexist.
5. Yes, because the reading passage quoted similar questions that Sally was asked by the press.
6. Yes. The reading indicated that reporters hounded her about being a woman and complained about not being able to get much information from her. The cartoonist shows her walking away from the reporters and refusing to answer their stupid questions.

4 Facts and Opinions

1. opinion	5. opinion	8. fact
2. fact	6. fact	9. opinion
3. fact	7. opinion	10. opinion
4. opinion		

5 The Prefix re-

1. reopen	5. rephrased	8. redouble
2. retracing	6. repossess	9. reclaim
3. reunion	7. reconstruct	10. revoking
4. recount		

6 Compound Words

1. daredevil, ripcord	5. heavyweight, roadwork
2. rosebush, tombstone	6. wardrobe, homecoming
3. tightwad, lookout	7. handyman, candlelight
4. windbreakers, motorboat	8. overjoyed, guesswork

Lesson 15

1 About the Reading

1. Opinion: They meant that they would make it to France or die in the attempt, but they didn't actually expect to see all the people in France or in heaven.
2. Fact: Harbo had felt the bump of a shark against the bottom of the boat.
3. Opinion: Harbo couldn't know ahead of time whether or not they could clear the giant wave, even though it turned out that he was right.
4. Opinion: The men were not intending to commit suicide.
5. Opinion: They thought they would earn a lot of money rowing across the ocean, but they were wrong.
6. Opinion: The reporter felt that Samuelson had been an unusually brave and adventurous man.

2 What Do You Think?

Answers will vary.

3 Synonyms

1. bulletin	5. furthermore	9. glorious
2. illegal	6. agreement	10. conflict
3. suspect	7. decrease	11. consideration
4. occupation	8. faraway	12. nerveless

4 Antonyms

1. ashore	5. disperse	9. remote
2. reckless	6. watertight	10. defense
3. irresponsible	7. abbreviate	11. inexperienced
4. retrieve	8. manmade	12. heavenly

5 The Prefix pre-

1. prejudged	5. preview	9. premedical
2. preheat	6. prewar	10. Prehistory
3. preschool	7. pretest	11. precooked
4. predated	8. preshrunk	12. prepay

6 Bodies of Water

1. A. sea
   B. lake
   C. river
   D. ocean

2.

Lakes	Oceans
Great Salt	Arctic
Huron	Atlantic
Louise	Indian
Michigan	Pacific
Rivers	**Seas**
Amazon	Caribbean
Mississippi	Dead
Nile	North
Snake	South China

3. a. the Nile
   b. the Pacific Ocean
   c. the Caribbean
   d. the Great Salt Lake
   e. Lake Louise

Review: Lessons 1–15

1 Word Review

1. capsule	6. Amazon	11. oilskin
2. morphine	7. satellite	12. reins
3. compass	8. myth	13. generation
4. megaphone	9. shuttle	14. Broadway
5. Nile	10. sextant	15. poverty

2 Word Review

1. d	6. b	11. d
2. b	7. b	12. a
3. d	8. a	13. d
4. c	9. a	14. d
5. c	10. d	15. b

3 How Would You Classify It?

1. astronaut	6. Cupid	11. moon
2. scarlet	7. sextant	12. *Challenger*
3. barrel	8. whale	13. cinnamon
4. rifle	9. encyclopedia	14. motorcycle
5. kerosene	10. cosmonaut	

4 Facts and Opinions

Answers will vary.

5 Review of the Apostrophe and Capitalization

1. Ever since she'd read the story of Cupid in her brother's Greek mythology book, Kate wished that such a god really did exist who would shoot an arrow of passion into Dr. Spring's heart.

2. "I'd meet you at Grand Central Station, but Manhattan's traffic is so bad you'd be better off just taking a taxi to West End Avenue," Adam told Aunt Mary, who was coming to visit for the weekend.

3. "They'll never have time to visit Grant's Tomb if they're planning to spend the afternoon in Central Park," said Tom who quickly added, "but then, who wants to see a tomb on such a glorious autumn afternoon."

4. After reading the article about Sally Ride's life in an old issue of *Time* magazine at the dentist's office, Tony was certain that her work on the *Challenger* had been much more relaxing than all the interviews she'd had to suffer through.

6 Five-Letter Words

MOORS 8 ROOMS	TUNAS 9 AUNTS	AMONG 1 MANGO	DREAD 16 ADDER
BELOW 2 ELBOW	FLIER 7 RIFLE	LEASE 15 EASEL	KNEAD 10 NAKED
HEART 11 EARTH	KNITS 14 STINK	RELAY 6 EARLY	LIVED 3 DEVIL
THORN 13 NORTH	ASIDE 4 IDEAS	RANGE 12 ANGER	BLEAT 5 TABLE

The world's largest inland sea: Mediterranean Sea

Lesson 16

1 About the Reading

1. b
2. b
3. c
4. a
5. d
6. a
7. c
8. b
9. a
10. d

2 A Recipe for Apple Fritters

1. Any five of the following: For, to, and, a, cast, fry, in, serve, it

2. A. take
   B. eggs
   C. batter
   D. pare
   E. cut
   F. them
   G. broad
   H. grease

3. A. fritters
   B. flour
   C. pepper
   D. make
   E. pieces
   F. fresh

4. Accept any reasonable guess, such as: There probably were no standard measurements at that time, or measuring cups and spoons were not available, etc.

5. Answers will vary.

3 Words with More Than One Meaning

1. a great number
2. a section of a hospital for the care of a particular group of patients
3. a group of assistants or workers
4. to question a sample group of people in order to survey public opinion
5. ghosts
6. to touch lightly in passing; to skim or brush
7. to annoy or upset
8. to put into action
9. a piece of such a material on which a painting is made, especially an oil painting
10. to give way to what is stronger or better

4 Wake Up and Smell the Coffee!

1. apples and oranges
2. rotten egg
3. in a nutshell
4. brownie points
5. in a pickle
6. carrot top
7. smart cookie
8. cost peanuts
9. couch potato
10. cream of the crop
11. a tough nut to crack
12. as easy as pie or a piece of cake
13. butterfingers
14. cool as a cucumber
15. egg on
16. two peas in a pod
17. forbidden fruit
18. from soup to nuts
19. go bananas
20. cry over spilt milk
21. big cheese
22. butter up
23. nest egg
24. nutty as a fruitcake
25. pie in the sky
26. a piece of cake or as easy as pie
27. the apple of one's eye
28. to have egg on one's face
29. don't upset the apple cart
30. walk on eggshells

5 Using the Apostrophe with Plural Words

1. the colonies' growth
2. the players' defense
3. the rascals' pranks
4. the skyscrapers' construction
5. the bananas' ripeness
6. the cartoonists' dismissal
7. the Canadians' friendliness
8. the rockets' red glare
9. the visitors' entertainment
10. the daredevils' boldness
11. the motors' roar
12. the nurses' availability

6 The Suffix -tion

1. accommodations
2. reservation
3. starvation
4. investigations
5. inflation
6. extractions
7. definitions
8. addiction
9. compositions
10. infections
11. exhaustion
12. explanations
13. temptation
14. graduation
15. combination

Lesson 17

1 According to the Author

a. Heartburn
   symptom: burning feeling in the chest
   cause: cigarettes, alcohol, rich foods, or overeating
   treatment: antacids, drugs, or surgery

b. Diarrhea
   symptom: frequent or runny bowel movements
   cause: virus
   treatment: drink liquids

c. Constipation
   symptom: infrequent or difficult bowel movements
   cause: lack of water and fiber in the diet or too many rich foods and processed sugars or medicine or stress
   treatment: healthy diet and exercise

2 About the Reading

1. All kinds of stress—emotional, mental, and physical—can have a negative impact on the digestive system.
2. Antibiotics are necessary to fight infections, but they can harm our bodies by killing off healthy bacteria.
3. Eating foods that are low in fiber, high in fat, and that contain refined carbohydrates can be disastrous for your digestive tract.
4. Medicines are good for us because they help us stay healthy, but they can also irritate the stomach lining and cause digestive troubles.

3 Using the Apostrophe with Plural Words

1. the chefs' recipes
2. the steel mills' output
3. the litterbugs' thoughtlessness
4. the strikers' settlement
5. the kittens' toys
6. the villagers' distrust
7. the roommates' possessions
8. the mountains' beauty
9. the researchers' findings
10. the sweethearts' affection

4 The Suffix -sion

1. division, profession
2. transfusion, permission
3. commission, conclusion
4. confusion, possession
5. impression, extension
6. revision, concussion
7. admission, invasion
8. omission, intermission
9. supervision, confession
10. transmission, decision

5 More Serious Problems of the Digestive System

1. Pain that starts around the belly button and moves to the lower right part of the abdomen.
2. It could burst, spreading bacteria into your abdomen. or It could kill you.
3. Pain on the lower left side could be from diverticulitis
4. Pain in the gut that moves to your chest or back; chills and sweating
5. The doctor will probably remove it.
6. No. Ulcers are caused by bacteria.
7. Both are treated with antibiotics
8. They are caused by bacteria.

Answers will vary on the last questions.

6 Word Review

1. Pacific
2. state
3. beaver
4. IOU
5. ulcer
6. mumps
7. cherries
8. digest
9. easel
10. foxhole
11. moon
12. oil
13. 1800s
14. Midas
15. help

Lesson 18

1 About the Scene

1. Answers will vary. Some students may feel that Ruth and Walter have a strong comfortable relationship, while others may think that their bickering is a symptom of a widening rift between them. Be sure students cite details that support their point of view.
2. Answers will vary. One possible answer is: She is strict but loving. She orders him to comb his hair and won't give him money for a cap, but she gives him a hug and words of playful affection.
3. Answers will vary. Accept any reasonable response.
4. Answers will vary. At the end of the play the family was moving to their own home. Ruth and Walter were expecting another baby and getting along better. However, since the entire play spans only a few weeks in their lives, any response that the student can justify is acceptable.

2 Food for Thought

1. c
2. d
3. c
4. d
5. b
6. a
7. c
8. a
9. c
10. d
11. c
12. c
13. a
14. a

Last question: brings home the bacon

3 Synonyms and Antonyms

1. introduction, conclusion
2. sudden, slow
3. affection, dislike
4. exasperated, contented
5. comical, tragic
6. minimum, maximum
7. extend, compress
8. masculine, feminine
9. gleeful, dejected
10. extract, insert
11. common, infrequent
12. broad, narrow

4 More Work with the Plural Possessive

1. cereal's, cereals'
2. frontiersman's, frontiersmen's
3. thief's, thieves'
4. foreigner's, foreigners'
5. utensil's, utensils'
6. child's, children's
7. McCormick's, McCormicks'
8. Congresswoman's, Congresswomen's
9. polisher's, polishers'
10. watermelon's, watermelons'
11. handyman's, handymen's
12. district's, districts'
13. reservation's, reservations'
14. axman's, axmen's
15. deer's, deer's

5 The Suffixes -ance and -ence

1. entrance
2. annoyance
3. substance
4. convenience
5. ignorance
6. importance
7. avoidance
8. resistance
9. confidence
10. riddance

Lesson 19

1 About the Reading

1. b
2. c
3. b
4. a
5. d
6. a
7. b
8. d
9. c
10. a
11. d
12. c
13. b
14. c

2 A Taste Test

Sweet
1. cheesecake
2. coffee cake
3. doughnuts
4. hot chocolate

Salty
1. bacon
2. cheeseburger
3. smoked ham
4. soy sauce

Bitter
1. baking chocolate
2. coffee
3. lemon peel
4. mustard greens

Sour
1. grapefruit
2. lime juice
3. sauerkraut
4. vinegar

Answers to the last two questions will vary.

3 Word Families

1. nutritious, nutrition, nutrients
2. entertainer, entertainment, entertain
3. convenience, conveniently, convenient
4. practically, impractical, practical
5. possessive, possessed, possession
6. confidential, confided, confidence
7. created, creator, creation, creative
8. obey, obedience, obedient, obediently
9. scientist, science, scientifically, scientific
10. indifference, indifferently, indifferent

4 What Do You Think?

1. Answers will vary. Accept any reasonable response.
2. Answers will vary.

5 Can You Crack the Code?

1. emerald
2. ruby
3. pearl
4. diamond
5. topaz
6. opal
7. sapphire
8. bloodstone
9. amethyst
10. garnet
11. turquoise
12. sardonyx

6 Review of the Apostrophe

1. cents' (second)
2. sausages' (second)
3. Scientists' (first)
4. days' (second)
5. trucker's (first)
6. warrior's (first)
7. Joneses' (second)
8. boy's (first)
9. noodles' (first)
10. gems' (second)

Lesson 20

1 About the Reading

1. he seemed to have a magical ability to understand plants and to develop useful products from ordinary plants.
2. they were considered good only as food for hogs.
3. they had never heard of them.
4. he wanted to serve his own people.
5. he was dressed cheaply and didn't look or act important.
6. he didn't want to profit from God's gifts.
7. Any three of the following or similar examples: He rejected a job at Iowa State and went to Tuskegee instead. He turned down high-paying jobs with Edison and Ford. He didn't apply for patents for his discoveries. He wore two-dollar suits.
8. Answers will vary. Accept any reasonable response.
9. they didn't understand the source from which his magic with plants came.
10. they believed they could and loved the plants enough.

2 More Facts about the Peanut

pods, usually, unusual, groundnuts
plants, temperature, period, ripened, snap, Pegs
ripen, plows, soil, machines
harvested, percent

3 Word Relationships

1. b
2. a
3. b
4. c
5. d
6. b
7. c
8. d
9. a
10. d

4 The Suffix -ize

1. specialize
2. modernize
3. tenderized
4. symbolize
5. memorize
6. recognize
7. organized
8. scandalized
9. terrorized
10. authorized
11. alphabetized
12. criticize

5 Find This Peanut Product

1. nostril
2. inhale
3. transfusion
4. ripcord
5. oxygen
6. gallbladder
7. laxative
8. yogurt
9. carbon dioxide
10. exhale
11. raisin
12. infection
13. navel

The peanut product: nitroglycerin

6 To Look at Any Thing

1. Most of us see only the surface of things, only the most obvious details or characteristics.
2. We must look at it long and become the thing, taking plenty of time to imagine ourselves as being the thing we are seeing.
3. Carver said, "The secrets are in the plants. To learn them, you have to love them enough." Accept other reasonable examples.
4. Answers will vary. Reasonable responses include: Learn from nature; isolate yourself while you study the thing you want to really know; read the Bible.

Review: Lessons 1–20

1 Word Review

1. preservative	6. profession	11. compatibility
2. patent	7. utensil	12. transmission
3. wizard	8. inflation	13. tradition
4. nutrient	9. frontier	14. agriculture
5. miracle	10. bureau	15. Senate

2 Which Word Does Not Fit?

1. windbreaker	6. salary	11. valued
2. deserve	7. Los Angeles	12. stunning
3. numb	8. hardworking	13. turnip
4. Mediterranean	9. reject	14. Franklin
5. starvation	10. plague	15. gold

3 Word Study

1. Plagued, nagging, endure, immediately, emergency
2. outraged, authorize, classified, creative, opportunities
3. scientist, assumed, concocted, assistant, explanation
4. advice, devise, device, advised, revise
5. desperate, dutiful, oppression, injected, foul
6. formally, formerly, confident, envy, detract
7. minimum, accommodate, maximum, limit, resume
8. unlike, unknown, unpleasant, unusually, unfruitful

4 Review of Compound Words

1. b	5. c	9. a
2. b	6. a	10. b
3. d	7. b	11. c
4. a	8. a	12. c

5 Review of Contractions

1. he's	8. won't	15. there's
2. they'll	9. she's	16. she'd
3. doesn't	10. you'll	17. I'm
4. we've	11. don't	18. let's
5. you'd	12. I'll	19. he'd
6. I'd	13. what's	20. ma'am
7. hadn't	14. they'd	

6 Review of Facts and Opinions

1. fact	5. opinion	9. fact
2. fact	6. fact	10. opinion
3. opinion	7. fact	11. fact
4. fact	8. fact	12. opinion